C000094543

A family tree

A family tree

The message of 1 Chronicles

Andrew Stewart

 EVANGELICAL PRESS

© Evangelical Press 1997. All rights reserved. No part of this publication may be reproduced, stored in a retrieval system or transmitted, in any form, or by any means, electronic, mechanical, photocopying, recording or otherwise, without the prior permission of the publishers.

First published 1997

British Library Cataloguing in Publication Data available

ISBN 0 85234 393 0

Unless otherwise indicated, Scripture quotations in this publication are from the Holy Bible, New International Version. Copyright © 1973, 1978, 1984, International Bible Society. Used by permission of Hodder & Stoughton, a member of the Hodder Headline Group. All rights reserved.

Printed and bound in Great Britain by
Creative Print and Design (Wales), Ebbw Vale

To my parents,
William and Margaret Stewart,
who first taught me about Jehovah,
the Lord God of Israel

Contents

Foreword

An essential requirement for anyone who would venture to write a Bible commentary is a constant remembrance of the Bible's own definition of what it is and what it does: 'All Scripture is God-breathed and is useful for teaching, rebuking, correcting and training in righteousness' (2 Tim. 3:16).

That awareness of Scripture and its purpose is clearly the hallmark of the fine series of Welwyn Commentaries published by Evangelical Press, and not least in this latest addition to their number, 1 Chronicles, by Andrew Stewart.

'All Scripture is ... useful...' Even the long lists of names in the first nine chapters of 1 Chronicles? With one of his many felicitous illustrations, Andrew Stewart answers, 'As we read through these lists, it is as though we are visiting a relative and are led into the best room to find that it is well stocked with family photographs. Along with each of those familiar faces there are memories to be cherished, lessons to be learned and debts to be acknowledged...' (p.22). And the admirably chosen title of his commentary, *A Family Tree,* follows through on that.

'All Scripture is God-breathed...' It is God's Word to us, and Mr Stewart's careful study of the text underlines the importance of knowing exactly what the written Word says. It is gratifying to his former Professor of Hebrew at the Reformed

Theological College, Belfast, to see that he uses careful word-studies not only to reach an accurate exegesis, but also, more unusually, a relevant application of Scripture.

'All Scripture is ... useful for teaching, rebuking, correcting and training in righteousness.' One is never allowed to forget that the Word is not only to be heard and understood, but is to be put into practice. Throughout, the Word is directly and insistently applied to the Christian and the church today. That kind of application must be made, for 1 Chronicles is not simply part of Old Testament history. King David pointed forward to 'great David's greater Son', and one of the outstanding merits of this book is the way in which the reader is constantly pointed to Christ.

To sum up, I found this most helpful commentary eminently readable, with excellent use of telling everyday illustrations, with pointed applications constantly made, good links with New Testament passages and, best of all, an interpretation that consistently pointed forward to Christ.

Hugh J. Blair
Emeritus Professor of Old Testament
Language and Literature
Reformed Theological College
Belfast
May 1997

Introduction
The historian as a theologian: the message of Chronicles

By any standards the book of Chronicles is an important part of the Old Testament. It is large, comparable with Isaiah or Jeremiah in size. Written as one book, it was first divided into two parts by the Alexandrian Jews who translated the Old Testament into Greek, producing a version of the Scriptures afterwards known as the Septuagint. Chronicles is a monumental history of God's people from the creation of the world until the edict of Cyrus in 538 B.C.

The book of Chronicles also marks the end of an era. Although it is to be found after the histories of Samuel and Kings in English versions of the Old Testament, it is the last book in the Hebrew canon (a fact testified to by our Lord's reference in Matthew 23:35 to the first and last acts of murder in the Hebrew Scriptures). It summarizes not only the history, but also the theology of the Old Testament — the revelation that God gave of himself at creation, to the patriarchs, through Moses, during the monarchy, exile and restoration.

The period after God's people returned from exile in Babylon was a fruitful one in terms of biblical theology. It is fascinating because in it the message of the Old Testament is most clearly and fully stated. The book of Chronicles was one of the most important writings from that period, so it is no

exaggeration to describe it as a summary of the message of the
Old Testament. Yet it is a book that is not appreciated by
Christian students of the Word as it ought to be. There are
several reasons why this might be so.

Firstly, *the Chronicler took a peculiar interest in matters
connected with the temple and the priesthood.* David and
Solomon are remembered not so much as statesmen, but as
builders of the temple and organizers of its staff. To many
modern Christians these are matters of little interest. The
liberal Anglican writer David L. Edwards writes, 'The Chronicler's view is so narrow that the Deuteronomist [i.e., the author
of the books of Samuel and Kings] appears in comparison a
large-hearted liberal... The Chronicler makes extensive quotations from five psalms, which he learned in the temple day by
day; but the grandeurs and miseries of the history of Israel are
seen remotely and vaguely, as if through a cloud of incense.'

This interest in the temple and its sacrifices was not
restricted to the Chronicler, for they are amongst the most
potent themes in biblical theology. It is the task of the preacher
and the student of Scripture to seek the key to unlock their
meaning. The writer to the Hebrews provides us with that key
in Hebrews 9:13-14: 'The blood of goats and bulls and the
ashes of a heifer sprinkled on those who are ceremonially
unclean sanctify them so that they are outwardly clean. How
much more, then, will the blood of Christ, who through the
eternal Spirit offered himself unblemished to God, cleanse our
consciences from acts that lead to death, so that we may serve
the living God!' Each one of the temple ceremonies described
in this book is a signpost guiding our thoughts to Calvary. Can
we possibly describe the Chronicler's history as being of little
interest to us?

Secondly, *the book of Chronicles is thought to be repetitive
of the history that we find in the books of Samuel and Kings*

(sometimes called the Deuteronomic history). This was obviously what the translators of the Septuagint thought when they took Chronicles from its position in the Writings and put it after Kings and gave it the title *Paraleipomenon*. This name means 'the things passed over', or 'the things forgotten', and implies that Chronicles is merely an appendix to the 'main' history of Israel which is to be found in the books of Samuel and Kings.

In fact the title given to Chronicles in the Septuagint is quite misleading. We find in the book of Chronicles several incidents that are not recorded in the earlier histories. Some of these give us significant insights into the reigns of important kings, such as Joash and Manasseh. The Chronicler's history is a vehicle for a number of extremely important themes, which he handles in a very distinctive way. It is important for us to remove our blinkers and take a fresh look at this portion of the Word of God.

Thirdly, *it has been alleged that the Chronicler is an inferior writer to the author of Samuel and Kings*. This is the thesis of Gerhard von Rad of Heidelberg. His contention is that the Chronicler gathered material previously written by the Deuteronomist and others and rearranged it to produce a devotional history, yet one that lacked depth and breadth: 'One cannot avoid the impression of a certain mental exhaustion at least in the way the material is presented. And in theological clarity too, in consistency and inner unity, the Chronicler is not nearly the equal of the Deuteronomic work.'

Once we begin our study of the text of Chronicles it will quickly become apparent that the Chronicler had a distinctive message, with a ready application to our own day. But what of the claim that as a writer he was stylistically inferior? The response of one who takes a conservative view of the inspiration and authority of Scripture is to ask, 'So what?' The Holy

Spirit is the divine author of the whole Bible, but he uses a variety of human authors to give us the Scriptures. These human authors bring their own backgrounds and training to bear on the way they write under the inspiration of the Holy Spirit. Mark was not as sophisticated in his use of the Greek language as was Luke 'the physician', but both wrote Gospels that are equally the Word of God. The same contrast can be drawn between the author of Samuel and Kings and the Chronicler, but as we study their writings we find that they both teach truths of great beauty and profundity.

It is important to recognize that Samuel-Kings and Chronicles are distinct and different works. They spring from very different situations. The books of Samuel and Kings were precipitated by the exile in 587 B.C., which was a cataclysmic disaster in the life of the covenant people and demanded some sort of explanation. Chronicles was written for the same nation after it had returned from exile, during a period of restoration and resettlement. As the Jews put down roots afresh, they were keen to learn what kind of a people they were, and what sort of a heritage was theirs. For this reason the writer of Samuel-Kings presents a great drama, working to a mighty climax, and emphasizes how God's judgement ran down the generations, until a day of disaster. His admitted literary genius has much scope with such a theme.

The purpose of the Chronicler is much more down-to-earth. He seeks to impress on the people their immediate duty to live godly lives, for blessing after obedience and punishment after disobedience are daily realities. He is less of a stylist and more of a pastor. The reader of his history will notice how extensively he quotes from prayers and sermons and records details of administration. He makes constant application of Israel's traditions to the daily life of God's people as they rebuild a shattered kingdom. There is, however, in both Samuel-Kings and Chronicles the same underlying message of a covenant God who provides salvation for his people, through a Redeemer or Messiah foreshadowed by the deliverer-kings whom God gave to his people.

Who was the Chronicler?

This question is linked to the question of date: when did the Chronicler write his history? The traditional view is that Ezra wrote Chronicles some time between 450-430 B.C., after his return to Judah in 458 B.C. His purpose in writing was to encourage the returning exiles in the work of rebuilding the temple. The evidence gathered to support this view can be summarized as follows:

1. The similarity between 2 Chronicles 36:22-23 and Ezra 1:1-4, both of which record the decree of Cyrus permitting the Jews to return to their homeland.
2. The interest that both Ezra and Chronicles take in the lineage and purity of the priests (see 1 Chron. 6; Ezra 2:62).
3. Both books regard the temple as of great importance in the life of God's covenant people.

It has even been argued that Chronicles, Ezra and Nehemiah originally formed a single work written by the one scribe, namely Ezra. This view has, however, to contend with the following objections:

1. It is far from proven that Ezra and Chronicles were originally two volumes of a single work. If so, why do they duplicate the edict of Cyrus and how did they come

to be separated in the Hebrew canon? It was the
Septuagint translators who brought them together, in
succession, as they now appear in our Bible versions.

2. In 1 Chronicles 3:19-24 it would appear that reference is made to the sixth generation after Zerubbabel,
the prince who went back with the first generation of returning Jews. This would suggest that the Chronicler
was probably writing after the time of Ezra.

The best conclusion to draw from the evidence available is
that Chronicles was written in the closing years of the fifth century B.C. by a Levite, otherwise unknown to us, and that his
purpose was to exhort his fellow Levites in their work and to
encourage the people of Judah to appreciate their heritage
from the Lord. As Malachi was to show, the fact that the temple
had been rebuilt did not guarantee that the priests and people
would continue to worship the Lord with all their hearts (Mal.
1:6-8; 2:1-9).

What do we find in Chronicles?

It is good to have in our minds a short summary of such a large
book when we come to study it. I like to think of the whole
work of the Chronicler (encompassing 1 and 2 Chronicles) as
a drama with an overture and four sections.

1. The overture (1 Chron. 1-9)

These chapters contain genealogies and lists of kings, warriors
and priests. This mass of data is used to introduce themes
which will be taken up and developed further in the ensuing
narratives. These lists emphasize continuity through the exile,

the preservation of a chosen nation and the centrality of two tribes in particular. The kingly tribe of Judah and the priestly tribe of Levi occupy most space in these chapters, focusing attention on the redemptive function of priest and king.

2. *The prelude* (1 Chron. 10-29)

These chapters cover the period of the early monarchy in Israel. The main focus is on the establishment of the kingdom under David. First of all, his enemies had to be defeated (chs 11,18-20), then an administration had to be established (chs 23-27). In the period of safety and security that followed he planned to build a temple for the Lord in Jerusalem (chs 28-29). In these chapters we become aware of the significance of this project in the history of God's people. The temple would be a place of worship that would bear the name of the Most High God; it would be an outward and magnificent sign of Israel's devotion to God. Yet David's part in this project would be a preparatory one.

3. *The climax* (2 Chron. 1-9)

It was not David, but Solomon his son, who was to build the temple for the Lord in Jerusalem. These chapters are the centrepiece of the Chronicler's history. 1 Chronicles looks forward to the day Solomon dedicated the temple, while the rest of 2 Chronicles looks back to that day and illustrates the lessons Solomon taught his people on that solemn religious occasion. When a nation honours God, God will bless it. The blessings that God poured upon Israel during the reign of Solomon are a testimony to that often-doubted truth. Solomon is a token of what God has done for his people and of what 'one greater than Solomon' will yet do for them.

4. The disintegration (2 Chron. 10 - 36:21)

These chapters detail the long, slow decline of Solomon's kingdom from its days of glory. They almost completely ignore the history of the northern kingdom of Israel. Not one of the northern kings could be described as 'good' and they are mentioned only as they affect the life of the southern kingdom of Judah. Even among the kings of Judah there is a sad story of spiritual decline. The principles of God's dealings with his people are set out with a simple clarity. Godly kings are blessed in their own lifetime, while ungodly kings are punished by being permitted to see the consequences of their ungodliness also in their own lifetime. A succession of bad kings led the nation to the disastrous exile of 587 B.C.

This steady decline was periodically arrested by godly kings, such as Hezekiah and Josiah, who called the people back to faithfulness to God's covenant of grace. God's covenant was an unchanging display of mercy, and these men sought the Lord. During their reigns periods of remarkable spiritual and national blessings were enjoyed, but succeeding generations quickly squandered any accumulated spiritual capital. Past blessing is never good cause for present complacency amongst the covenant people of God. Unfaithfulness called down the curses of that same covenant until the people were finally removed from the land in chapter 36.

5. The restoration (2 Chron. 36:22-23)

These verses record the decree of King Cyrus in 538 B.C. that the Jews in exile were to return to Jerusalem to rebuild the city. It is not on a note of destruction, but of restoration, that the Chronicler ends his history. The working of God's providence in history speaks of his sovereign mercy to undeserving men and women. Even a pagan ruler like Cyrus was an instrument in God's hands and a shepherd for the flock of God (see Isa. 44:24 - 45:3).

This is also a Messianic note on which to end. The Lord's anointed will be a mighty king who will deliver his people. Like the rest of the Old Testament, the Chronicler leaves us with the hope of a Saviour who will provide deliverance for his people. 'But when the time had fully come, God sent his Son, born of a woman, born under the law, to redeem those under law that we might receive the full rights of sons' (Gal. 4:4-6).

1.
A world stage

Please read 1 Chronicles 1:1-54

Washington D.C. is a city of many monuments. One of the most interesting is the black marble memorial to the 58,156 Americans who died in the Vietnam War. It takes the form of a simple marble wall and only as you approach it do you see what makes it so striking. The names of all the American servicemen and women who died in that war are engraved onto the marble, and the list of names seems to stretch into the distance. There is a solemn atmosphere at this memorial as visitors scan the wall for the name of a friend or loved one and memories flood back.

The book of Chronicles (I say 'book' because although we think of two books of Chronicles, they were originally penned as one) is a monument to the battles of a spiritual superpower. Although the nation of Israel was never large by the standards of today, she was loved by God and occupied a special place in his purposes of grace (see Deut. 7:7-8). Her laws disclosed God's holiness; her prophets foretold a great deliverer; her kings hinted at an everlasting kingdom; and her priests pointed to a sacrifice that would bring an end to all blood-shedding. This history book is a monument to the triumphant grace of God.

As the book of Chronicles charts the development of God's gracious plans it introduces us to many human players in the drama. We shall find long lists of priests and Levites, sons and daughters, wives, workers and kings. This is especially true of the first nine chapters of 1 Chronicles. As we begin our study of this book we are struck by its rather unusual introduction. The book begins with a list of names: **'Adam, Seth, Enosh, Kenan, Mahalel, Jared, Enoch, Methuselah, Lamech, Noah'** (1:1-3).

To people from Western cultures this might seem a rather off-putting introduction to a book, more reminiscent of an electoral register than of Scripture. Yet for cultures with a stronger emphasis on family roots such lists have a ready message. As we read through these lists, it is as though we are visiting a relative and are led into the best room to find that it is well stocked with family photographs. Along with each of those familiar faces there are memories to be cherished, lessons to be learned and debts to be acknowledged, and the cumulative effect is a sense of belonging and blessing.

When we read the list of names in this chapter we read our own family tree — whatever our racial origin. This is not exclusively Jewish; it is also universal history. Adam and Noah are fathers of us all. The families of Noah's three sons are listed in verses 4-27. The last-mentioned and most famous of Shem's descendants was Abraham (1:27). His family is listed in 1:28-37, in three sections according to his three wives, Hagar, Keturah and Sarah. Abraham is the spiritual father of all those whose faith rests in the Lord Jesus Christ (Gal. 3:29). Among Abraham's physical descendants were some who did not share his faith in God, and in 1:38-54 the Edomites, or the descendants of Esau, are listed.

As well as the godly, the ungodly are mentioned in this chapter. As well as the great men, there are the otherwise unheard-of men whose lives are brought to bear upon our own by this inspired historian. Let us consider what lessons these lists contain for us.

People are important

As we read through the lists of names in chapter 1, some of them grab our attention. There are the great figures of Old Testament history, like Adam, Noah, Abraham, Esau and Israel. These men are like milestones in the history of God's dealings with men and women, marking out failures and new beginnings. Adam was the first man, and in Genesis 2:15-17 we read of God entering into a covenant with him. Adam broke the covenant (Hosea 6:7), but that fall into sin became the occasion when God unveiled his gracious promise of a Saviour (Gen. 3:15). Noah was the man who saw God destroy the human race by a flood. God preserved only Noah and his family, and then re-established his covenant with all creation (Gen. 9:8-17). Noah is an appropriate figure to refer back to in this chapter because God's covenant with him reminds us that God is Lord of the whole earth, and not just one nation. As we have seen, Abraham was the father of the faithful and when God renewed his covenant with Abraham he gave the promise of many descendants and a fruitful homeland (Gen. 12:2-4).

As well as these 'fathers of the covenant', this chapter mentions some who live on in the names of the nations they established. There is Javan (1:5), who was the father of the Greeks, and in 1:7 we read of Tarshish (Spain) and Kittim (Cyprus). Then there are Cush, or Ethiopia (1:8,9,10), Mizraim (1:8,11), whose name is the Hebrew word for Egypt, and Canaan (1:8,13). Some of the names mentioned called for special comment, such as Nimrod (1:10), Peleg (1:19) and Hadad (1:50-51). Most, however, were just ordinary people about whom we know little more than that they existed. The only other reference to them in Scripture is in the genealogies in Genesis from which our Chronicler most probably derived his information (Gen. 5:1-32; 10:1-32; 11:10-27; 25:1-26; 36:1-43). Yet God the Holy Spirit worked in the mind and heart of the Chronicler to preserve their memory like that of many 'unknown warriors'.

Scripture has much to say about the worth of people created by God (Gen. 1:26-27; 2:15; Ps. 8:3-8; James 3:9). God made men and women as individuals, giving them personality, individuality and dignity, and giving their service significance within his overarching purposes. Even in heaven, when all God's people are gathered together, they will be remembered by name (Rev. 2:17). This chapter also teaches us that God places people in a community where they are bound by ties of kinship which bring privilege and responsibility. John Donne made this point when he wrote that 'No man is an island.' Our Chronicler makes the same point as a historian, with his emphasis on family lists.

All humanity is God's stage

Notice how the focus of the chapter narrows as we read it. The chapter begins with Adam, the father of all men, and finishes by focusing on the family of Israel. Along the way it has passed several important forks in the family tree. The first came in the time of Noah, when the flood reduced the whole of mankind to three families, the descendants of Shem, Ham and Japheth (Gen. 6:5-8). Of these three families, the family of Shem is the one that most occupies our attention because Abraham came from that family. Abraham's sons are listed in 1:28-34, but only one was the son of promise, and that was Isaac. Of Isaac's two sons it was Jacob who received the blessing. As we follow these forks in the family tree we are able to trace the covenant line of blessing.

Our focus narrows because God sets his love on an elect people. This is one of the great themes of biblical history. The

God of the Bible is a sovereign God and his free choice determines who will be among his redeemed people (Gen. 18:18-19; Deut. 14:2; Amos 3:2; Mal. 1:2-3).

In the New Testament the apostle Paul responded to the complaint that it is unfair of God to choose one and pass over another: 'Does not the potter have the right to make out of the same lump of clay some pottery for noble purposes and some for common use?' (Rom. 9:21). As we read through the history of Israel and Judah we shall see that in every age God has chosen some whom he will preserve for himself. At times this was a very small remnant, and at others it was a large empire. Throughout every age in history God is the Lord of all, and all humanity is involved in his plans to display his power and mercy. The centre of this history is not the affairs of one nation, but the doings of the God who made and governs all. That is why it starts, not with David, Moses or Solomon, but with Adam.

Hostility faces God's people

Just because the Lord is sovereign does not mean that his people will always have an easy life. The picture that this history gives of the covenant people should disabuse us of that naïve suggestion. This first chapter, and especially verses 38-51, reminds us that the people of God were surrounded by enemies.

Isaac's rejected son was called Esau and even though he did not appreciate his birthright as the elder son (Gen. 25:29-34), he resented losing it to his deceitful younger brother Jacob (here in 1:34 referred to by his God-given name of Israel — see Gen. 27:41; Heb. 12:16-17). Esau's jealousy left a legacy of bitterness that was to be directed against Israel for generations to come. The Edomites (as the descendants of Esau came to be known) attacked the Israelites when they came to possess the promised land (Num. 20:14-21). They gloated as Nebuchadnezzar attacked Jerusalem in 587 B.C. and even struck down the terrified fugitives as they escaped (Obad. 10-14). The Edomites certainly merited the vengeance of God (see Ps. 137:7-9).

The sons of Esau are listed in 1:35-42. They also became known as the people of Seir — Seir being one of Esau's descendants who gave his name to the mountain strongholds where his people lived. This rival kingdom was well organized. It had kings long before a king ruled in Israel (1:43). These kings had cities, which were a sign of wealth and power, and they were able to dominate their neighbours — including for a time the people of Israel. As a testimony to the power of this kingdom, the Chronicler lists the succession of Edomite chiefs (1:51-54).

Although this rival kingdom had stolen a march on the people of Israel and for a time was able to threaten the covenant people of God, we must note its frailty. The Chronicler draws his information about the Edomite rulers from Genesis 36, but he adds a note of his own telling us in verse 51 that **'Hadad also died.'** Powerful though he was in his day, Hadad was only a man whose kingdom was built on the strength of flesh and blood. Just as Hadad died, so too did his kingdom. All other earthly kingdoms will face the same fate, but God's kingdom is an *everlasting* kingdom. Let us therefore remember the words of Psalm 47:7-9 when we face hostility from those in the world amongst whom we live and witness:

> For God is the King of all the earth;
>   sing to him a psalm of praise.
> God reigns over the nations;
>   God is seated on his holy throne.

The nobles of the nations assemble
   as the people of the God of Abraham,
for the kings of the earth belong to God;
   he is greatly exalted.

2.
Judah: the royal tribe

Please read 1 Chronicles 2:1 - 4:23

The abiding phrase from George Orwell's novel *Animal Farm* is the slogan announced by Napoleon the pig that 'All animals are equal, but some are more equal than others.' It is a fact borne out by experience that some people are more likely to rise to positions of prominence and privilege than others. In every society there seems to be some sort of natural 'aristocracy'. The same was true even amongst the people of God in the Old Testament, for God in his wisdom raised some to positions of special responsibility.

By the time that the Chronicler wrote his history of God's people it was clear that although there were twelve tribes in Israel, some were of greater importance than others, and especially that Judah was no ordinary tribe. He begins this section with a list of Jacob's twelve sons, who were the patriarchs of the twelve tribes of Israel. Interestingly, the list we find in 2:1-2 starts in the same order as in Genesis 35:23-26, where Moses lists the families who went with Jacob when he returned to Bethel (in the land of promise) after his stay in Paddan Aram, but when the Chronicler expands his list to outline the descendants of the patriarchs pride of place goes not to Reuben, the firstborn, but to Judah.

The people of Judah

Judah had the largest population of all the tribes, inhabited the largest territory and figures most prominently in the history that will be unfolded in the book of Chronicles. In the family tree of Judah we meet many interesting and important people who left their mark on the nation's history. These heroes are what made Judah such an important tribe, and the significance of Judah is emphasized by the wealth of information we have about these people. Let us consider some of them.

Wise men

In 2:6 **'Ethan, Heman, Calcol and Darda'** are mentioned. They also figure in the account of Solomon's reign given in 1 Kings 4:31 for these were some of the wise men who surrounded the king. Even a king like Solomon, who was known for his great wisdom, felt the need to surround himself with good and wise men to protect himself from making foolish mistakes. Solomon himself acknowledged the importance of such men: 'Plans fail for lack of counsel, but with many advisers they succeed' (Prov. 15:22). How much more ought we to appreciate, and even seek out from others, the counsel that will restrain our foolish inclinations!

Black sheep

Some members of the tribe of Judah did not bring honour to their tribe, but trouble. In 2:7 the Achan who brought defeat and tragedy to the whole nation of Israel at the battle of Ai (see Josh. 7) is mentioned. Here he is known appropriately by the name **'Achar'**, which means 'trouble'. He disobeyed God by

stealing from Jericho some of the treasure which had been
devoted to God, the token of which was to be its total
destruction (Josh. 6:17-18,21). This is an Old Testament idea
that we shall meet again in 4:41.

Godly men

In 2:10-12 we come to that part of the line of Judah that
included Boaz, the great-grandfather of King David. His
genealogy is already recorded for us in Ruth 4:18-22. In that
beautiful little book we read of the kindness of Boaz to Naomi,
another member of the tribe of Judah, and her Moabite
daughter-in-law, Ruth. Boaz noted Ruth's plight and, as well
as showing a very practical concern for her material needs, he
sought to act as her kinsman-redeemer. He protected her,
while maintaining her purity and increasing her happiness.
The mention of such individuals within the tribe of Judah
reminds us that it is from this tribe that God planned to bring
forth one who is 'holy, harmless and undefiled' and who will
be the Kinsman-Redeemer for his people (Isa. 11:1).

Prominent men

The family line of Boaz leads us to the high point in the
genealogy of the tribe of Judah. The fact that Judah brought
forth the royal line of King David accounts for the prominence
it is given by the Chronicler. Of all the many branches of the
line of Judah it is in the branch of David that he is most
interested. The family of David's father Jesse is listed in 2:13-
15, including the older and stronger brothers who were passed
over in favour of the youngest and least experienced. We are
reminded that it is not because of our worthiness that God calls
us into his service, but because of our calling God equips us so
that we are fitted for his service.

Other members of David's family are named in 2:16-17. Here we read the names of his sisters and their sons, who became powerful players in the turbulent politics of David's reign (see 2 Sam. 3:39). Their methods and priorities were not those of the godly King David, and we see a graphic illustration of how men so closely linked by blood and background can have very different attitudes to the things of God. We can never presume that the privilege of coming from a godly family will make our lives any less prone to sin and temptation.

In 3:1-24 the Chronicler focuses more particularly on the family of David. His sons are listed, as is the royal line from Solomon to the exile and beyond. There are nineteen generations until the exile and a further eight thereafter, making this the longest and most significant family line in these opening chapters.

Gifted men

In 2:18-20 the family of **'Caleb son of Hezron'** is mentioned. This man is to be distinguished from that other, more famous, Caleb, the son of Jephunneh. Caleb's line leads up to the name of **'Bezalel'** the craftsman in 2:20. He was not the only craftsman in the tribe of Judah, for we read in 4:21 and 23 of linen-workers and potters. It is not just kings, royal advisers and generals who deserve mention in this roll of honour, but any person who uses the talents that God has given him or her in the service of God.

Bezalel, however, deserves special notice and would have been of great interest to the Chronicler because he was the master craftsman who made the furnishings for the tabernacle in the days of Moses (Exod. 31:1-11). Although it was Moses, a member of the tribe of Levi, who received instructions for constructing the tabernacle, and it was the Levites who were charged by God with the responsibility of ministering in it, the

tribe of Judah had an honourable role in providing this place
of atonement through which the people drew near to God.

David and Solomon would later follow in the footsteps of
Bezalel when they sought to build the temple in Jerusalem as
the place to which the tribes of Israel could come to seek the
Lord. We also know that it was to be an even greater branch of
the tribe of Judah (Heb. 7:14) who would open 'a new and
living way' to God, not by embroidering curtains or fittings,
but by tearing apart a veil of separation so that blood-cleansed
sinners might enter in (see Matt. 27:51; Heb. 10:19-20).

Courageous men

In 4:15 the better-known Caleb, the son of Jephunneh, is
mentioned. He is one of the great heroes of the Bible, for he
served the Lord 'wholeheartedly' and that is a quality greatly
prized by our historian. Of the twelve spies who surveyed the
promised land in Numbers 13 only Joshua and Caleb brought
back a good report because in faith they knew that God is as
good as his promises and that the land was already theirs if they
would only take it. Right into old age this faith and enthusiasm
marked all that Caleb did for the Lord.

Ordinary men

Most of the people mentioned in the family lists of 1 Chronicles 2:1 - 4:23, and especially those of 4:1-23, are ordinary
people who would otherwise be completely unknown to us. A
little background information is given about some (e.g. Jabez)
but all we know about the others is that they lived and plied
their various trades — scribes, linen workers, potters, crafts-
men and soldiers.

Among God's people there is great dignity in work and
labour, whether that is leading armies, running the government,

selling cloth or making household goods, and our work is to be done as unto the Lord (Eph. 6:7). For these people it was an honour to be recorded in Scripture as those who **'stayed ... and worked for the king'** (4:23). May people see us as men and women who dedicate our talents, however meagre we may think them to be, to the service of an even greater King.

Lessons we can learn from the history of Judah

1. Unfaithfulness brings terrible consequences but it does not result in the destruction of God's people

Oliver Cromwell once asked for his portrait to be painted 'warts and all'. The Chronicler paints a very honest picture of this most important of the tribes of Israel, even to the point of recording in its family lists some very unflattering references that do not appear in the main historical narrative. It is not true to claim, as some do, that the book of Chronicles gives us a sanitized version of Israel's history. The family lists of Israel's premier tribe abound with hints of failure, and in each case it should be noted that failure bought pain and shame in its wake.

The far from faultless family life of Judah and his sons is hinted at in 2:3-5 (see also Gen. 38:1-30). Judah sinfully married a Canaanite woman called Bathshua (or daughter of Shua). His sons by Bathshua behaved shamefully and provoked God to show in a very clear way that 'The wages of sin is death', and only by an incestuous relationship with his daughter-in-law Tamar was Judah's family line continued at all.

Other shameful incidents are referred to directly or hinted at in the list of Judah's descendants. Achar — better known as Achan — brought the conquest of the promised land to a standstill until his sin was discovered and punished (Josh. 7:1-

26). Even King David, whose name and family dominate this chapter, and from whose family the Messiah was to come, came to a time of painful failure when he sinned by committing adultery with Bathsheba. The sons she gave to David are listed in 3:5, where she is known by the Hebrew name Bathshua. It seems that by using this form of the name (which has un- savoury connotations in the light of 2:3) the Chronicler is showing that the sins of the past will come back to haunt the house of Judah!

It is also interesting to note that one of the four sons born to David and Bathsheba was called Nathan (3:5). This was the name of the prophet who had rebuked David for his sin and warned him that the son conceived through his adultery would die in infancy. Nathan's rebuke brought home to David the awfulness of his sin and plunged him into the depths of despair. His faithful words wounded David sorely and they showed him that sin has crippling effects even in the lives of God's people. David was gracious enough to listen to Nathan, and from the fact that he named a subsequent son by Bathsheba after him, it would seem that he learned from him. Here are two marks of godly character — the ability to speak the truth in love (Eph. 4:15; Prov. 9:8-9) and the ability to take a rebuke.

The lesson, however, that the Chronicler is most keen to apply to his readers is that sin brings painful consequences in the lives of those who commit it. God's people must never be allowed to think that they are free to sin and forget the consequences, just because God is gracious. Unfaithfulness is a serious matter and brings severe consequences, but it does not destroy God's purposes of grace. We note that the two blemishes in the family line of Judah did not prevent it from becoming the lineage of our Lord and Saviour Jesus Christ. Indeed they are also recorded by Matthew in his genealogy of our Lord (Matt. 1:3,6), for 'Where sin increased, grace in- creased all the more' (Rom. 5:20).

2. Faithfulness is the key to enjoying God's continued blessing

As well as providing examples of unfaithfulness, the line of
Judah furnishes us with some fine examples of faithfulness.
There was Caleb the son of Jephunneh, who along with Joshua
brought back the report that the promised land was a good land
and encouraged the people to go into it in the confidence that
God would be faithful to his promises (Num. 13:30). Even at
the age of eighty-five he was a warrior for the Lord, making the
bold claim before capturing Hebron: 'Now give me this hill
country that the Lord promised me...The Lord helping me, I
will drive [the Anakites] out just as he said' (Josh. 14:12).

A life of faith leaves a legacy of blessing for those who
follow, as can be seen in the family line of King David. David
was outstanding as a man of faith, and that is how this history
presents him. The Chronicler shows David to be a very human
figure, but one of great faith. Our abiding image of him is to
be found in 17:23-27, where we see him submitting to God's
plans for his family. David was confident of the blessing that
would pass down the generations of his family and in Hebrews
11:32 he is named as one of the heroes of faith.

God blessed David's life of faithfulness by placing twenty-
one of his direct descendants on the throne of Israel and Judah.
Even after the exile had obliterated many other family records,
the family line of David is recorded through a further eight
generations until the time that the Chronicler wrote. One
commentator writes of this list that it is 'suggestively lengthy
and tantalizingly cryptic'. Some Jews after the exile had hoped
that Zerubbabel (3:19) would be the promised Messianic King
(see Hag. 2:23; Zech. 4:7-10). But the Chronicler gave them
no encouragement to cherish that hope. What he did show was
that God had preserved the royal line of Judah. God's promises
had not been extinguished and at any moment he could raise
up deliverance for his people. What an encouragement to

God's faithful, praying people to cry out day and night for God to redeem his people for the sake of his glory!

Faithfulness is a vital element in the prayer life of God's people and there is an honourable, though often overlooked, example of believing prayer in the example of Jabez in 4:9-10. We are told that Jabez stood out from his contemporaries as a man of prayer. As a prayer warrior he shows us what blessings we so often forfeit when we do not take an issue to the Lord in prayer. Let us consider his circumstances, his confidence and his petition.

His circumstances. Jabez did not have to seek his sorrows. The abiding memory that his mother had of the day he was born was one of unusual pain in childbirth. She **'gave birth to him in pain'** and it is most probable that without modern medical techniques Jabez carried into boyhood, and even adult life, the physical scars of that day — possibly a withered limb or a hunched back. His name — which means 'pain' — may have been a cruel taunt among the boys with whom he played as a child. These are the hurtful circumstances in which Jabez cried to God.

His confidence. Jabez did not cry out to some deity or 'god out there', as many irreligious people do in time of trouble. He did not cry out to a stranger, but to the covenant God of Israel, who had revealed himself in the Scriptures and whom Jabez honoured and loved. That is the title Jabez gave to God in 4:10, and the words of the prayer that followed are emphatic: **'Oh, that blessing you would bless me!'** These words echo the promise that God had made to Abraham in Genesis 12:2 and 22:17. Jabez's confidence was grounded on what he had discovered of the faithfulness of God, both by special revelation and (we may presume) by personal experience.

His petition. Jabez's prayer arose out of his circumstances. After all, as the *Westminster Shorter Catechism* teaches, 'Prayer is an offering up of our desires unto God,' and Jabez brought to God the desires that burdened him most. He sought release from his physical pain. He also sought the strength that he needed to serve God by possessing the land that had been promised to Israel. His prayer was that God would enlarge his territory. We should not think that Jabez's prayer was too mundane or too selfish. There is nothing wrong in praying for physical health and earthly blessing so long as we recognize that it may not be God's will to grant us all we seek, and so long as we realize that such physical and material gifts are useless without corresponding spiritual blessings. Jabez sought these too when he prayed to God, **'Let your hand be with me, and keep me from harm.'** These words breathe the spirit of Moses as he prayed in Exodus 33:15: 'If your Presence does not go with us, do not send us up from here.' Jabez sought to walk with God, and subdue the territory of the land that God had promised to his people for his own glory.

3. Outsiders are incorporated into the tribe of Judah

Although this is the family line of those descended from Judah, from time to time the entry of 'new blood' into the tribe is noted. In 2:34 we read of Sheshan, who had no sons, giving one of his daughters in marriage to his Egyptian servant Jahra so that his family line might continue. This was an example of how an outsider came into the line of God's people as a convert from the heathen world. Also in 4:17-19 we read of a man called Mered marrying an Egyptian princess. As there is no hint in either of these cases of shame or reproach we can assume that there was genuine conversion to the God of Israel as well as incorporation into the people of Israel, as happened in the case of Ruth the Moabitess, who also entered the tribe of Judah (see Ruth 1:16-17).

Perhaps the most significant addition to the tribe of Judah that is recorded in these chapters is the family of Jephunneh. From Numbers 32:12 we know that this family was of Kenizzite stock, one of the peoples that had lived in Canaan before the Israelites entered the land as conquerors. Yet we find that a scion of this line was Caleb, the great warrior and example of faith whose example we have noted already.

Here is a notable illustration of the great biblical doctrine of adoption which was given such full expression by Paul in Ephesians 2:11-13: 'Therefore, remember that formerly you who are Gentiles by birth and called "uncircumcised" by those who call themselves "the circumcision" ... you were separate from Christ, excluded from citizenship in Israel and foreigners to the covenants of promise, without hope and without God in the world. But now in Christ Jesus you who once were far away have been brought near through the blood of Christ.'

3.
The frontier tribes

Please read 1 Chronicles 4:24 - 5:26

Life on the frontier has exercised a powerful attraction for many people through the centuries. Thousands have left security at home to go to America, Africa or Australia to settle on the frontier, with its promise of land, opportunity and challenge. There is much that is exciting and romantic as well as daunting and dangerous. The passage that we study in this chapter turns our attention to the four frontier tribes of Israel: Simeon in the south; Reuben, Gad and Eastern Manasseh to the east.

Three features are to be found in the short descriptions given by the Chronicler of these tribal groups. We are given genealogical information showing how the tribes grew, geographical information showing how their territory expanded and military information showing how they lived. Life on the frontier was marked by conflict, but also by excitement and victory over the enemies of God's people.

Simeon (4:24-43)

Simeon was one of the smaller tribes in Israel. Only one family line is recorded in this section (4:24-27) and we are told that **'Their entire clan did not become as numerous as the people of Judah'** (4:27). Simeon lived in the south of the promised land towards the Negev desert. Their main town was Beersheba and others are listed in 4:28-33. These towns were part of the territory originally allocated to Judah at the time of the conquest of Canaan (Josh. 15:28-32), but because Judah's portion was larger than its population could occupy this most southerly part of it was given to the tribe of Simeon (Josh. 19:1-9). Consequently Simeon existed in Judah's shadow, eventually being incorporated into the structure of Israel's premier tribe.

What contributed most to the diminution of Simeon's status as a tribe by comparison with the rest was its division and scattering, as prophesied by Jacob in Genesis 49:7: 'I will scatter them in Jacob and disperse them in Israel.' This was the punishment that resulted from the violent sins of Jacob's two sons Simeon and Levi, although its effects were more devastating for the descendants of Simeon than for those of Levi. Those Simeonites who lived in the towns mentioned in verses 28-31 continued there until the time of David, when Simeon joined the tribes that rejected the house of David. As David was the champion of the tribe of Judah these Simeonites were no doubt unwelcome in the territory of Judah, and so they were scattered throughout the rest of the northern part of the kingdom.

Other Simeonites remained loyal to the house of David and they retained their identity as a sub-group within Judah. They were even given an honourable mention in the history of Judah, fighting side by side with their brethren in the southern kingdom during the reign of King Hezekiah. Their exploits are described in 4:41 and they are shown to have been zealous in the service of the Lord.

These Simeonites who were loyal to the house of King David led the expansion of the southern kingdom into neighbouring areas. They were God's instruments in bringing about an answer to Jabez's prayer of 4:10. Men of prayer like Jabez are important members of the community of God's people, for without them nothing of lasting value is possible, but it is also important to have men of action like the Simeonites who were prepared to shed their blood and sweat to achieve the extension of God's kingdom. 'Expect great things from God,' advised the great missionary pioneer William Carey, but he also encouraged us to 'Attempt great things for God.' These are two aspects of Christian service that must never be separated.

Expansion to the west took the Simeonites to Gedor (or Gaza) and into the territory of the Philistines (4:39). To the south-east this expansionist move took them into the land of the Meunites, who were Arabs or descendants of Ishmael (4:41), the land of the Edomites, who had their mountain stronghold at Mount Seir (4:42), as well as the territory of the Amalekites (4:43). Several conflicts with the Meunites are mentioned later in the book of Chronicles, but verse 41 refers to an outbreak of hostilities during the reign of King Hezekiah that is not otherwise mentioned in Scripture.

A distinctive quality marked these skirmishes on Israel's borders. The Simeonites were seizing the land that God had promised to his people many years earlier so that it might be dedicated to him. The verb *charam,* or 'destroy', used in verse 41 is a strong one, which originally conveyed the idea of prohibition. Holy things in Israel were solemnly set aside to God so that they could not be put to common use because they were consecrated to God (Lev. 27:28-29). The word came to have a special significance during the conquest of the promised land in the time of Joshua, indicating that God had commanded something to be dedicated to him by total destruction. It was used to describe the destruction of the treasures of Jericho when the people of Israel captured it (Josh. 6:17-18,21; cf. Micah 5:9). This is the sense in which it was used by the Chronicler in 4:41. By this action the men of Simeon were also removing from before God's eyes the defilement of their heathen practices, cleansing the land and returning it to the Lord who is its ultimate owner according to Psalm 24:1.

The significance of this method of claiming the land for God has perplexed many Christians over the centuries. That God is the Lord of the whole earth is not to be doubted by his people, and that he visits his wrath upon the wicked in time as well as in eternity is also taught in Scripture. The question remains: how far ought men to go in enforcing God's rule by the power of the sword? (Rom. 13:4; Matt. 5:39; 26:52). The church does not have any authority to inflict civil punishment, for it is by the influence of godly living and gospel preaching that she seeks the glory of her King and Saviour. What we also know is that God's people must show no tolerance for evil in their hearts, lives or churches. The Septuagint translation of this verse uses the Greek verb from which we get the word anathema: 'They anathematized them.' The New Testament teaches us a similar intolerance of evil (see Mark 9:43-47; Gal. 1:9; 1 Cor. 5:7,9,13).

We should also notice that blessing came to the section of the scattered tribe of Simeon that stayed amongst people who loved the Lord and served his anointed king. The company we habitually keep will have a profound effect on the lives we lead and the characters we develop. While the company of godly people encourages faithfulness and brings blessing, friendship with the world is a very different matter (see James 4:4) and the consequences are disastrous.

Reuben (5:1-10)

Although Reuben was the firstborn amongst Jacob's sons (2:1) his tribe is listed third in this series of family lists. We are told the reason for this in 5:1-2. Apart from the incestuous and immoral nature of Reuben's sin, the effect of his action in sleeping with Bilhah, his father's concubine (Gen. 35:22; 49:4), was to lay claim to his father's authority and wealth (see other examples in 2 Sam. 16:21-22; 1 Kings 2:13-23). The fifth commandment, as well as the seventh, was infringed by this incident! The result was that Reuben was demoted from his entitlement to a double blessing and it was shared between Joseph's two sons, who had been adopted by Jacob as his own (Gen. 48:5). As a result Ephraim and Manasseh stand as patriarchs in Israel and as heads of their respective tribes.

The grim spectre of the exile is also raised by the list in 5:4-6. These verses list a line of Reubenites right down to Beerah who was carried into exile by the Assyrian king, Tiglath-Pileser, in 733 B.C.

During the time between entering the land and the exile the Reubenites enjoyed great blessing. Their territory was expanded to include large tracts to the east of the River Jordan, from the edge of Moabite territory (Aroer and Nebo) northwards into Gilead, and eastwards into the desert beyond which lay the Euphrates river (5:7-9). Gilead was a land made prosperous by cattle-rearing and became famous for its wealth (Gen. 37:25; Jer. 46:11). God gave the Reubenites this land by giving them victory over its previous inhabitants, the Hagrites (5:10,19-21). These were Arabs descended from Hagar, Sarah's handmaid who bore Ishmael as a son for Abraham (Gen. 21:14). Because Ishmael was not the son to receive the blessings of God's promise Hagar and her son were put out from Abraham's household and a bitter hostility developed. The Hagrites are mentioned in Psalm 83:6 as traditional enemies of Israel, typical of those who plot against God and his people. Here is a reminder that those whom God curses no man can bless, but those whom God blesses no man can destroy.

Gad (5:11-22)

Even though they were one of the northern tribes and did not join with Judah in the southern kingdom, Gad knew a measure of God's blessing. Their families are listed in 5:11-15 and their territories in 5:16. As well as inhabiting the northern part of the fertile land of Gilead, they occupied Bashan to the north, where the rich pasturelands were renowned for rearing live-stock (see Ps. 22:12). The census on which these reports are based was taken during the reigns of Jotham King of Judah and Jeroboam II King of Israel which, materially speaking, were regarded as a golden age in the history of Israel. This was probably the high-water mark of the tribe of Gad as well.

In co-operation with their fellow Israelites in the tribes of Reuben and Eastern Manasseh the men of Gad were able to put an impressive army into the field (5:18) and so to face greater enemies than the Reubenites had fought on their own (5:19). Yet our historian is at pains to point out that their victory was not won by military strength alone. These Israelites were strengthened by God. They did not trust in their own strength, but cried out to the Lord for help (5:20).

In giving these tribes the victory over their enemies the Lord was giving them the promised land in fulfilment of his covenant promise that he would give them a place of safety in which to serve him alone. That is why the Chronicler reminds us that **'The battle was God's'** (5:22). The list of plunder gathered after the victory is a visible symbol of the blessings that the Lord gives to those who cast themselves upon his mercies. Great are the blessings which go to those who fight and win the victory in God's strength.

Eastern Manasseh (5:23-26)

Without giving a list of descendants to illustrate his point, our historian describes the numerical growth of this half of the tribe of Manasseh that settled east of Jordan (5:23). They settled in the land of Bashan to the north of that portion of Bashan occupied by the tribe of Gad.

The only list of names that we have is in 5:24, which names the family heads in this tribe. We note that these were gifted men, yet their great gifts of character, physical strength and leadership could be of no lasting value where God's blessing was forfeited (see Ps. 20:7-8; 118:8-9). The final verses of this chapter give a warning to balance the teaching of 5:20-22. They show what happens when people are not faithful and do not seek the Lord. Unfortunately these verses also provide the most fitting words to conclude the account of these northern tribes.

These frontier tribes, including Eastern Manasseh, were unfaithful to God in a very serious way. Their idolatry is described as a form of prostitution (5:25). Frequently in the Old Testament this is how the prophets spoke of the sin of idolatry (e.g. Ezek. 23; Hosea 2). For people who had been consecrated to the Lord to put anyone or anything in the place of God was not just to slight his honour, but also to violate his covenant with them. God had joined himself to his people in a union akin to that between husband and wife, so to worship other gods was to engage in spiritual adultery. These sins are described in very graphic language in verse 25, as too is God's reaction in verse 26.

Another vivid phrase is used in 5:26 to describe how God punished their unfaithfulness: **'So the God of Israel stirred up the spirit of Pul king of Assyria.'** This describes how God intervenes in the affairs of men. God stirred up the spirits (or the hearts, since the heart is regarded as the seat of human motivation) of men to bless his people — as he did in the case of Cyrus, to send the Judean exiles home (Ezra 1:1), and in the case of Zerubbabel and Joshua the high priest to rebuild the temple once they had returned home (Hag. 1:14). God also stirred up the hearts of men to bring calamity upon his people. The exile was such a calamity — an act of divine justice (Zech. 1:12). Heathen kings were the tools that God used, but it was

God who stirred up their hearts so that his covenant-breaking people might be punished. Their plight was the result of provocation and a refusal to repent and seek forgiveness. As a result these tribes, unlike Judah, which had sought forgiveness, were still in the bondage of exile.

The conflict continues

The victories and progress of these rugged frontiersmen ought to be of interest to modern Christians. Our lives may have many more material comforts, but we are still exposed to the attacks of those who are hostile to God and his kingdom. God has not taken us out of a hostile world, but placed us in its midst as warriors for Christ (John 17:14-15; Eph. 6:10-13).

The struggle in which we are engaged is one that we cannot fight on our own. Our natural gifts of stamina, intelligence, experience or ability to lead others will never be enough without the spiritual gifts that flow from God's grace. 'The weapons we fight with are not the weapons of the world... We demolish arguments and every pretension that sets itself up against the knowledge of God, and we take captive every thought to make it obedient to Christ' (2 Cor. 10:4-5; cf. Eph. 6:14-18).

The assurance that our spiritual battles are the Lord's is a great consolation to the Christian believer. It also causes us to examine our hearts. Matthew Henry comments, 'If the battle be the Lord's, then there is reason to hope that it will be won.' That sentence begins with an important 'if...' Too easily can hurt pride or frustrated ambition make us aggressive and turn our energies into conflict with fellow believers. We think and act like worldly people because we want our own way to prevail and can easily persuade ourselves that some selfish action is in reality motivated by zeal for God. What a careful watch we must keep on the motivation of our own hearts!

How great are the blessings of those who truly and faithfully serve on the Lord's side! The men of these tribes fought hard battles, but they won a great inheritance. Consider too the promise of our Lord to the church in Ephesus: 'To him who overcomes, I will give the right to eat from the tree of life, which is in the paradise of God' (Rev. 2:7).

4.
Levi: the priestly tribe

Please read 1 Chronicles 6:1-81

Of all the tribes of Israel, the Levites had the greatest reason to be interested in genealogies. Although the punishment of their father Levi's sin had been that his descendants would be scattered throughout Israel (Gen. 49:7), God turned this into a blessing. Levi became the priestly tribe, with an influence that spread throughout the whole nation of Israel. With this unique position came many privileges and responsibilities. Malachi even spoke of a special covenant with the tribe of Levi (Mal. 2:4-6). The privileges of this covenant were limited very strictly to the descendants of Levi, and the right to minister at the altar was restricted to the descendants of Aaron. Priests were allowed to eat as food the flesh of sacrificial animals not consumed on the altar (Lev. 22:10-16). But only Levites who could *prove* that they were from the line of Aaron were admitted to these privileges (see Ezra 2:62-63). Family history was therefore of more than antiquarian interest.

This chapter, which records genealogical and other information about the tribe of Levi, recognized this concern of the Levites to preserve the identity of their families, but is obviously more than a database for those who wanted to research their ancestry. The information we find recorded here is selective and at times lacking in detail. The Chronicler's purpose is to use his distinctive historical style to sketch the history of this tribe and indicate its significance in God's plan of salvation for his people.

Levi was obviously an important tribe. After Judah they are given the greatest amount of space in these introductory chapters. This tribe lies at the centre of these family lists in chapters 1-9 just as the tabernacle and temple in which the Levites served lay at the centre of the spiritual life of God's people. We shall notice several features peculiar to the tribe of Levi.

A hope of deliverance that stretched into the exile and beyond (6:1-15)

These verses list the line of Levi, through his second son Kohath, down to Aaron and the sons who succeeded him as priests in Israel. Apart from the sons of David who continued the royal line, this is the only family line that stretches without interruption from the patriarchs to the exile. Just as the family of David gave the tribe of Judah great significance as the royal tribe, so the family of Aaron gave the tribe of Levi similar significance as the priestly tribe.

Both priestly and kingly functions are central to God's plan of salvation. The distinctive contribution of the Reformation to our understanding of the work of Christ was the Reformers' depiction of his three offices — that is, the three aspects of our Lord's work of salvation. This is summarized in the answer given to question 23 of the *Westminster Shorter Catechism*: 'Christ, as our Redeemer, executeth the offices of a prophet, of a priest, and of a king, both in his estate of humiliation and exaltation.' The Chronicler anticipates this emphasis by bringing together the tribes of Judah and Levi, whose distinctive roles had been kept so strictly apart throughout the history of the Old Testament (see 1 Sam. 13:8-14; 2 Chron. 26:16). Attention in the early genealogies of 1 Chronicles focuses on the kingly and priestly lines and in subtle ways our historian weaves together these two strands of the covenant people, all the time looking forward to the salvation that comes through the one who is both a King and a Priest for ever. The prophet Zechariah shared this hope and linked it to the promised Messiah (Zech. 6:13).

There were, however, imperfections amongst the human priests mentioned by the Chronicler in this list. In 6:3 we read of Aaron's two oldest sons, Nadab and Abihu, who 'offered unauthorized fire before the Lord, contrary to his command' (Lev. 10:1-3) in the exercise of their holy duties. Because they added to God's express commands they provoked a fearful display of his anger and were thereby blotted from the priestly line. Their younger brother Eleazar continued the family line and served as high priest.

There are also significant omissions from the list given here. There is, for instance, no mention of Eli, who was the high priest at Shiloh towards the end of the period of the judges, nor of his wicked sons Hophni and Phinehas. Neither is there any reference to Uriah who, at the request of King Ahaz of Judah, built a replica of the pagan altar that he had seen in Damascus and erected it in the temple of the Lord in Jerusalem (2 Kings 16:10-16). Unfaithfulness among spiritual leaders is an especially serious sin with many hurtful consequences for God's people, and we are reminded that God demands exemplary conduct from those who are in positions of leadership.

We are also reminded that even where its functions were exercised by sincere and upright men, the Aaronic priesthood was never able to make other needy sinners perfect before God

(Heb. 8:7-12; 10:1-4). The writer of the letter to the Hebrews teaches that the priesthood of Christ is far superior because he 'has become a priest not on the basis of a regulation as to his ancestry but on the basis of the power of an indestructible life' (Heb. 7:16).

An interesting pattern marks this list of names from Aaron to Jehozadak in 6:3-15. The men named are those who held the office of high priest, serving in the tabernacle and then in the temple. The centrepiece of the Chronicler's history and theology is the building of the temple in Jerusalem during the reign of King Solomon. From Aaron down to Azariah, **'who served as priest in the temple Solomon built in Jerusalem'** (6:10) there are twelve generations. Twelve is a number that signifies completeness amongst the people of God. Yet from Azariah to that other event which was of great significance for the Chronicler — the return from the exile and beginning to rebuild the temple — only ten generations are recorded. This lack of symmetry is an important feature of the list, for this list of priests is incomplete.

The list finishes in 6:15 with Jehozadak, whose son was Joshua, the high priest who had worked with Zerubbabel to restore true worship in the temple after the exile (Hag. 1:1-2; 2:1-5; Ezra 3:2). This Joshua was also known to Zechariah (see Zech. 3:1-9; 6:11) and may have been a kinsman of Ezra the scribe (Ezra 7:1-6). Although our historian would have had the information to hand, he does not bring his list to a balanced conclusion — twelve generations between Solomon's temple and the restored temple after the exile. That would have been to celebrate the restoration after the exile too much.

God's great deliverance of his people was not to be found in the restoration of animal sacrifices in an earthly temple at the centre of a merely earthly kingdom. Rather the history of salvation proclaimed in the Old Testament reaches its climax when the Son of God, whose kingdom is not of this earth (John 18:36), made the sacrifice of himself and entered heaven to make everlasting intercession for his people (Heb. 9:24-28). The very gaps of Old Testament history are a blessed testimony to one 'who comes in the name of the Lord' (Ps. 118:26).

A special witness to God's grace (6:16-53)

In this section four distinct family groups within the tribe of Levi are mentioned: the family of Gershon (6:20-21), the family of Kohath (6:22-28), the family of Merari (6:29-30) and the family of Aaron (6:50-53). Apart from these families there is a brief reference to other Levites who were assigned to various duties (6:48).

Just as in a beehive each member of the hive has its work assigned to it, so each member of the tribe of Levi had a particular task assigned by God. Some were given a special ministry of organizing the temple music, and one of the distinctive features of the Chronicler's history is the special mention made of their work. They were not self-appointed musicians following the dictates of popular taste and fashion. Rather, they **'performed their duties according to the regulations laid down for them'** by David the servant of the Lord (6:32; cf. 25:1-31).

David's influence on the organization of the temple was profound. Significantly the family lists of 6:16-30,50-53 trace the descent of the Levites only as far as the time of David and Solomon, when the worship of the Israelites was thoroughly reorganized and the temple was built (6:31-32), because to the Chronicler this was the golden age of God's activity from which we are to learn many lessons. These lists are supplemented later in chapters 23-27.

Three outstanding figures were appointed by David to organize the worship of God's people: Heman, Asaph and Ethan. As well as training singers and leading the nation in praise to God, these men and their sons left behind them songs of praise that have been preserved for us in the book of Psalms. Heman wrote Psalm 88, Asaph Psalms 73-83, the sons of Korah (6:22,37) Psalms 84-85 and Ethan Psalm 89. In these psalms we have a rich spiritual treasury and the purpose of the lists in 6:33-46 is to establish the legitimacy of these three musical families (Kohathites in verses 33-38, Gershonites in verses 39-43 and Merarites in verses 44-47). As descendants of Levi and men appointed by King David, who was responsible for the spiritual as well as the political leadership of the Old Testament people of God, their work established a pattern which was intended to exercise a lasting influence upon the worship of God's people.

Pride of place in these family lists, however, is reserved for the house of Aaron. While David had organized the temple musicians and other functionaries, Aaron and his descendants had an even more ancient commission. Their ministry had been given to them many years earlier **'in accordance with all that Moses the servant of God had commanded'** (6:49), and was the ministry of offering sacrifices at the altar. It was this task that set them apart from the other Levites, because Aaron's descendants stood as priests between a holy God and a sinful nation. Their ministry pointed to the peculiar privilege of God's people in every age — that a way of atonement has been provided so that even as unworthy sinners they might come to God for forgiveness and rejoice in the assurance that both they and their prayers are made acceptable to God through the shedding of sacrificial blood.

A ministry spread throughout the whole nation of Israel (6:54-81)

We have seen that the scattering of the tribe of Levi was originally a punishment (Gen. 49:5-7), but it turned out to be a blessing. A tribe of people devoted to serving God was spread throughout the nation of Israel, and in return for their spiritual ministry the other tribes ministered to the material needs of the Levites. The other Israelite tribes were given portions of the promised land on condition that a tenth, or a tithe, be returned to God. This tithe was to support the Levites, who would then devote themselves to the holy work to which God had called them. These other tribes were to allocate from their portions towns in which the Levites might live — on average four towns from each tribe.

The extent of the scattering of the Levites throughout the promised land is indicated in 6:55-81, where the towns allocated to the Levite clans by the other tribes in Israel are listed. A similar list is to be found in Joshua 21:8-42, the main difference being that the information in 1 Chronicles 6 is arranged so as to give greater prominence to the family of Aaron. Recognition is hereby given to the principle that those who serve God in spiritual affairs are to be supported materially by God's people (cf. 1 Cor. 9:13-14; 1 Tim. 5:17-18).

Through their scattering the Levites were to be a leavening and blessed influence throughout the land of Israel. Linked so closely to the house of David during the time of the monarchy, they also exercised a unifying influence among tribes that were often suspicious of royal authority (see 2 Sam. 20:1-2; 1 Kings 12:16-17). They had charge of at least one of the cities of refuge to which an unwitting sinner might come for safety from the law, which cried out for his blood. In this way they bore testimony to the mercy of the God of Israel. Their main influence, however, was to preserve revealed truth and true worship.

In every corner of the land there were to be pockets of godly men and women who would not be carried away by the often prevailing winds of apostasy that swept many throughout Israel into indifference or idolatry. One such was the family of Elkanah (6:27-28), who is described in 1 Samuel 1:1 as an Ephraimite. He was a Levite living in the hill country of Ephraim, where his clan had been allotted its place to live (6:67). Year after year he and his family went up to the tabernacle at Shiloh to keep faith with God. His wife Hannah was an especially noteworthy example of a godly wife. When unable to bear children she prayed earnestly to the Lord about her distress and, as we read in 1 Samuel 1:1 - 2:11, the Lord answered her prayer. Out of this home came Samuel, the last of the judges and the first of the prophets, the man who anointed the first two kings of Israel, and whose life brought great blessing to all Israel (1 Sam. 3:19-21).

Samuel is an example of what every Levite ought to have been. God's purpose in setting the Levites aside for his service was not that they might become religious recluses engrossed with the conduct of empty ritual, but that by the lives they led and the words they spoke they might teach the people the great truths about God and his way of reconciliation with sinners (Mal. 2:10).

Here too is an example for every child of God. God has not saved us to rest contentedly and complacently within the comfort of our families and fellowships. Rather we are to be scattered in the world around us as salt and light. God has given us work to do. He has given us neighbours to live beside, and the test of our Christianity is whether our lives and lips convey to them the truth of salvation that causes men and women to glorify our heavenly Father.

5.
All Israel

Please read 1 Chronicles 7:1 - 9:44

These chapters are perhaps the most difficult section of the book of Chronicles to summarize. Like many loose threads woven together, they produce a quite unique and sometimes puzzling design. It is as though the Chronicler has gathered together every last piece of information that his researches into Israel's history have brought to light and, however trivial they might appear, recorded them for future generations. We should not imagine, however, that he was careless in selecting material to include in these chapters, for the key to understanding them is their very inclusiveness: **'All Israel was listed in the genealogies in the book of the kings of Israel'** (9:1).

The two words **'all Israel'** summarize the genealogical history of God's people contained in 1 Chronicles 1-9, and indicate the Chronicler's purpose in them. Before seeking to learn the lessons he would have us learn, let us summarize the information he gives us.

The remaining tribes of Israel (7:1-40)

Six comparatively short tribal lists are given here: Issachar (7:1-5), Benjamin (7:6-12), Naphtali (7:13), Manasseh (7:14-19), Ephraim (7:20-29) and Asher (7:30-40). These tribes were allocated land west of the Jordan and were part of the northern kingdom of Israel. An interesting feature of these lists (with the exception of Naphtali, Manasseh and Ephraim) is that the number of fighting men ready for battle is recorded. These figures may have been obtained from the census that took place early in David's reign when he was joined by the followers of Saul's dynasty to form one united nation of Israel (12:1-38), or from the ill-fated census that brought disaster (21:1-7). Either way, we note that God's people are to be prepared people, always ready to serve their King, whatever the circumstances (see Neh. 4:16-18; Eph. 6:11,13).

It would appear that the Chronicler had a special interest in the families and place-names mentioned in these chapters. He wrote his history as an encouragement to those families, mostly from Judah and Benjamin, but also from all the tribes of Israel, who returned to the promised land after the exile. Not every branch of these tribes is recorded, but in all probability it is the forebears of those who returned who are singled out for the record. Although those who returned to Judah faced ridicule and hostility from many quarters (see Neh. 4:1-2; 6:1-19), the Chronicler reminds them that they were not foreigners or usurpers, but men and women of faith who were claiming the inheritance that God had promised to his people.

Ezer and Elead are mentioned in 7:21-22, by way of a warning, as men who tried to claim the promised land ahead of God's time. They were sons of Ephraim who lived in Egypt with the children of Israel during their slavery there. They would not wait for God to lead his people back to the land of promise and launched a raiding party of their own, discovering to their cost that 'Those who live by the sword shall die by the sword.' Pre-empting God's plans is never a sign of faith, but is disobedience and signifies a lack of faith in God's ability to work out all things for the good of his people. Those who had returned to Jerusalem to resettle the land of promise were by contrast living in a day when God was giving his people the opportunity to reclaim their covenant inheritance.

With the addition of these tribal lists the number of tribes mentioned reaches the ideal figure of twelve, based on the twelve sons of Israel. Although Zebulun and Dan are mentioned as Israel's sons in 2:1, there are no lists of their descendants recorded in the subsequent chapters. It is possible that 7:12 may list members of the tribe of Dan. This suggestion is based on a comparison with Genesis 46:23. A more likely suggestion is that some tribes dwindled to the point where they ceased to be reckoned as tribes with an independent existence and were assimilated into others. With the division of Joseph's descendants into the two tribes of Ephraim and Manasseh and the further division of Manasseh into eastern and western sections, the total number of tribal units remained constant at twelve.

Various listings of Israelite tribes are given in the Old Testament (see Gen. 35; Num. 1; 1 Chron. 27), but the symbolism of twelve as the number of tribes that comprises the whole nation of Israel remained intact. Here the complete list is as follows: Judah, Simeon, Reuben, Gad, Eastern Manasseh, Levi, Issachar, Benjamin, Naphtali, Western Manasseh, Ephraim and Asher. In spite of all their unfaithfulness and in spite of all that had befallen these northern tribes, God's covenant with all Israel stood firm.

The tribe of Benjamin (8:1-40; 9:35-44)

Although they are listed with other tribes in 7:6-12, a special reference is made to the tribe of Benjamin in chapter 8 and again at the end of chapter 9. The amount of information given about this tribe calls for some comment as only the tribal lists for Judah and Levi occupy more space. Benjamin was Judah's partner in the southern kingdom, and the Benjamites (together with the tribes of Judah and Levi) were one of the major groups in the population after the return from exile. As has been suggested earlier, the Chronicler's interest in the past is shaped by the pastoral needs and concerns of the generation of Jews who had returned after the exile. This explains the special interest taken in Judah, Levi and now Benjamin. Significantly, the list of Benjamite chiefs in 8:1-28 concludes with the note that **'They lived in Jerusalem'** — the place to which the exiles returned.

Another, and even more important, reason why the tribe of Benjamin is given such attention is the fact that it was the tribe of Saul, Israel's first king. The genealogy of Saul's family is singled out for special mention in 8:29-40 and is repeated word for word in 9:35-44 as a prologue to the account of the king's death in chapter 10. Although Saul's reign started with great promise, it came to be remembered as a false start for the Israelite monarchy. It was an example of how the Lord's anointed should *not* reign. In a subsequent chapter we shall consider some of Saul's mistakes and how his unfaithfulness brought terrible consequences both for himself and his descendants. Before considering the terrible warnings from Saul's example, the Chronicler reminds us that God does 'not stay angry for ever but delight[s] to show mercy' (Micah 7:18; Ps. 103:9). When God moved to restore his people to their promised inheritance, even the descendants of Saul were amongst 'all Israel'.

Resettling Jerusalem (9:1-34)

As the Chronicler drew the family lists of the tribes of Israel to a conclusion, he brought them to life by showing how they related to those who had returned from the exile. The people

listed in 1 Chronicles 2-8 were not just men and women who
had lived and died and passed into history. They were people
whose lives and struggles had brought a living nation into
existence and by God's grace that nation was living again in
Jerusalem. 'All Israel' is listed throughout its generations as a
prelude to the message that 'all Israel' will be redeemed and
restored as the covenant people of God.

First to return to their property were the groups mentioned
in 9:2. **'Israelites'** was a broad term encompassing people not
just from Judah and Benjamin (the two tribes of the southern
kingdom), but also from Ephraim and Manasseh (two tribes
which came to represent the tribes of the northern kingdom).
Unfaithfulness and idolatry were not sins peculiar to any one
tribe or group of people (Rom. 3:19). Not only had Benjamin
been tainted by the sins of Saul, and the northern tribes by their
rebellion against David's house and years of apostasy, but
Judah too had been **'taken captive to Babylon because of
their unfaithfulness'** (9:1). Now, however, God's purposes
of grace were reasserting themselves in his restoration of 'all
Israel' to the promised land (9:3-9).

Special attention is given to the tribe of Levi in this chapter.
The priests are listed in verses 10-13, Levites who were
'temple servants' in verses 14-16 and the gatekeepers in
verses 17-32, while musicians are mentioned in verse 33. We
shall consider the gatekeepers further when we come to chapter 26, where a further list is given. Here the record describes
their work (9:24-32) and the importance of their office. They
were first organized by Phinehas, who played an important
role in Israel's history during the time in the wilderness (9:20).
His zeal to purge idolatry from the nation's life is described in
Numbers 25:6-13 and Psalm 106:28-31. Centuries later David
and Samuel confirmed their service at the time when the
Levites were reorganized with the establishment of Jerusalem

as the central place of true worship. After the exile and the restoration of the Jerusalem temple their work was needed again. Theirs is a record of faithful service over many centuries — a glorious heritage to record!

The Chronicler was keen to remind the people who had returned to Jerusalem that they must not waste the opportunity now being offered to them. If their only concern was to reoccupy their homes and farms in the land of Canaan, they would repeat the mistakes of their fathers that had brought the exile upon them as a punishment from God. God's purpose in bringing them back was not simply to reinhabit the land, but to restore the hearts of the people to God and to re-establish true worship. In these plans the leadership and teaching ministry of the Levites were vital elements.

Now let us turn to see some of the lessons in God's grace that we can draw from these chapters.

The continuity of God's covenant promises

In spite of all the sin that this history records, God would not abandon the promises that he had made to his chosen people. Neither the sins of the patriarchs, nor the failings of the kings, neither the rebellion of the northern tribes, nor the hypocrisy of those in the south, nor even the idolatry of the priests could cause God to abandon his people. No, God's plan of salvation stands firm. So often the history of Israel illustrates the principle that Paul set out in Romans 5:20: 'Where sin increased, grace increased all the more.' Paul saw that principle brought to its New Testament conclusion on the cross at Calvary, 'so that, just as sin reigned in death, so also grace might reign through righteousness to bring eternal life through Jesus Christ our Lord' (Rom. 5:21).

The Old Testament also teaches the indestructibility of God's covenant love. Ephraim, the tribe specifically mentioned in 9:3, tested God's patience to its limits, but saw the triumph of grace:

> 'Is not Ephraim my dear son,
>   the child in whom I delight?
> Though I often speak against him,
>   I still remember him.
> Therefore my heart yearns for him;
>   I have great compassion for him,'
>
> > > declares the Lord
> > > (Jer. 31:20).

> How can I give you up, Ephraim?
>   How can I hand you over, Israel?
> How can I treat you like Admah?
>   How can I make you like Zeboiim?
> My heart is changed within me;
>   all my compassion is aroused.
> I will not carry out my fierce anger,
>   nor will I turn and devastate Ephraim.
> For I am God, and not man—
>   the Holy One among you
>
> > > (Hosea 11:8-9).

Then too, the conclusion of the Chronicler's narrative reminds us that deliverance from the pain of the exile was offered to all who would go up to Jerusalem (2 Chron. 36:23). Yes, even then there was mercy for Ephraim, just as today there is salvation for men and women of every nation who will believe on the Lord Jesus Christ and be saved.

The completeness of God's covenant people

The frequent and detailed references to the northern tribes in these chapters balance the Chronicler's concentration on the affairs of the tribe of Judah. The covenant people included all Israel! The northern tribes were not forgotten when Hezekiah called the nation back to God in his time (2 Chron. 30:5,10-12,18-20). They were also part of the restored community after the return from exile (9:3).

In New Testament times we read of members of these tribes who loved the Lord and looked for his Messiah. One of those who gave thanks for the birth of our Lord was the prophetess Anna, who was from the tribe of Asher (Luke 2:36-38). When John the apostle, in his heavenly vision, heard the number of those sealed for salvation he noted that there were 12,000 from each of the twelve tribes of Israel (Rev. 7:4-8). Here John drew on the Old Testament teaching that not one segment of God's people would be lost, but that all Israel will be saved.

In Romans 11 Paul developed this teaching so as to reassure believers in the church at Rome who were fearful that the extension of the gospel to the Gentiles might be to the spiritual detriment of the Jews. No, Paul emphasized, for God's purposes in election stand firm: 'For God's gifts and his call are irrevocable' (Rom. 11:29). 'Israel has experienced a hardening in part until the full number of the Gentiles has come in. And so all Israel will be saved' (Rom. 11:25-26).

We can draw great blessing for our souls from the assurance that no segment and no individual member of God's covenant people will be cast off. God's election is not only *from* eternity; it is also *unto* eternity, and its blessings are everlasting. Our Lord rejoiced in that as he prayed his great high-priestly prayer: 'None has been lost except the one doomed to destruction' (John 17:12). We too can rejoice in the assurance that this gives to every believing child of God because our Lord also said, 'No one can snatch them out of my Father's hand' (John 10:28). Rather, we can be 'confident of this, that he who began a good work in you will carry it on to completion until the day of Christ Jesus' (Phil. 1:6). We can also rejoice in the promise that this gives to the evangelistic mission of the church, for God's chosen people are now scattered through not just the twelve tribes of Israel, but every nation under heaven (see Rev. 5:9; 7:9-10).

The centrepiece of God's covenant plan

Jerusalem is one of the world's great cities. For centuries it has captured the imagination of those who live in it or lay claim to it. Even in recent history blood has been shed to hold sway over Jerusalem. In Bible times it was a unifying focus among the tribes of Israel (see 8:28,32; Ps. 122; 137:5-6). Jerusalem was the centre — even the symbol — of the promised land and it was the place to which the tribes returned.

In 1 Chronicles 9 we have a picture of the restored community living together in the shadow of the rebuilt temple. The temple dominated not just the city's skyline, but the lives of its people. It gave this community a very strong identity as the people of the Lord, for Israel after the exile was a priestly nation shorn of any pretence of imperial greatness. In this new situation, the temple and its ministry came increasingly to the fore as the centrepiece of God's plans, speaking of better things to come.

The new Jerusalem after the exile became a symbol of the grace that would go out to all nations (Micah 4:1-2). Jerusalem would set the stage for a great work of redemption that would reach its climax when our Lord Jesus Christ died at Calvary, just outside Jerusalem. His sacrifice did away with the temple sacrifices for ever and from Jerusalem the gospel of free forgiveness through his blood went out to every nation on earth (Acts 1:4,8). At the centre of the lives of those saved through his blood there will be the person of Jesus Christ, our great High Priest. Yet in the preparatory times of the Old Testament, before these things were understood clearly, it was the temple that stood at the visible heart of the piety of God's people.

When John the apostle recorded in the book of Revelation the great climax of God's plan of redemption, he saw 'the Holy City, the new Jerusalem, coming down out of heaven' (Rev. 21:2). As John looked more closely, he 'did not see a temple in the city, because the Lord God Almighty and the Lamb are its temple. The city does not need the sun or moon to shine on it, for the glory of God gives it light, and the Lamb is its lamp' (Rev. 21:22-23). Samuel Rutherford echoed those verses as he said on his deathbed, 'The Lamb, the Lamb has all the glory in Immanuel's land.' Do we know the truth of this in our lives? Do we truly glory in the work of Christ for us? Do we give him and his work the place that is due to him in our thoughts, prayers and worship? For he is the centrepiece of our salvation.

6.
The death of King Saul

Please read 1 Chronicles 10:1-14

Sellar and Yeatman in their satirical history of England, *1066 and All That*, reduce the great figures of English history to one-word assessments — either good or bad. Oliver Cromwell, for instance, is described as 'a good man but a bad thing'! In this chapter the Chronicler's account of the life and reign of Israel's first king is so compressed that it might be summed up in one inevitable fact: he died!

There is so much that a historian might have said about such an important figure in the history of Israel. Saul reigned for forty-two years (1 Sam. 13:1), longer than the reigns of David and Solomon, and that in itself makes him one of the most important Israelite kings. He set a new pattern, being Israel's first king. He led many military campaigns and he left his mark on the history of the whole region. That Saul is not an unimportant figure is demonstrated by the fact that no less than twenty-three chapters of 1 Samuel describe his life and reign (1 Sam. 9-31), but the Chronicler appears to view him as one of the lesser characters of the Bible. We are told that he lived, we are given some details of his life and then we are told that he died.

The reason why 1 Chronicles records Saul's life as it does is not because Saul was considered to be an insignificant figure, but because his reign did not touch very directly on the great interest of our historian — the temple (or its forerunner the tabernacle) and its ministry. In Saul's time the tabernacle was still in use — a mobile structure in which the ark of the covenant was kept. Saul showed disinterest bordering on contempt towards the tabernacle and its sacrifices (e.g. 1 Sam. 13:9), so it is not surprising that little of a positive nature is recorded about him in this chapter. The fact that occupies our attention is that he died to make way for David's accession to the throne.

In modern times the subject of death has become one of the great taboos in popular culture. That has not always been the case. In Victorian times death was openly discussed, invitations were even sent to funerals and extensive reports on funeral processions were carried in local newspapers. Now that progress in medical science has made many once-deadly illnesses curable we are much less willing to consider the reality of death. Yet the Bible has much to say about it: death is a dark valley (Ps. 23:4); it is the wages of sin (Rom. 6:23); it is a messenger from God; it is a certainty (Heb. 9:27). We can put it out of our minds for a time, as Saul sought to do, but we cannot avoid it for ever. That is the lesson we learn from the dark and tragic life of King Saul.

Saul had lived as a man of war, often facing the Philistines in battle. This chapter describes how he fought his last battle against the Philistines on Mount Gilboa, south of the Jezreel valley above Beth Shan (10:1). The Philistines had penetrated deep into Israelite territory and that day defeated the armies of Israel. Knowing what the Philistines would do to him if they caught him alive, Saul asked his armour-bearer to take his life and when the armour-bearer refused the king committed suicide. Yet even from the events of that dark day there are important lessons to consider.

The honour Saul received at his death

In spite of all the wrong that he had done Saul was honoured
by those closest to him, and his memory was treated with
respect. The much fuller account of Saul's life in 1 Samuel is
not a flattering one, showing us what a monster he had
degenerated into, threatening the lives of those who served
him (even his own sons). Yet in this account of Saul's death
there are elements of the narrative that are sympathetic, and at
times even touching. It is not simply that the Chronicler speaks
well of the dead, for he records some indications of the loyalty
Saul still commanded even as his kingdom collapsed into
military defeat.

Saul was honoured as a *father*, dying with his sons at his
side: **'So Saul and his three sons died, and all his house died
together'** (10:6; cf. 10:2). Literally, the Hebrew says they died
'as one'. This is not saying Saul's whole family was extermi-
nated that day. Obviously that was not the case, because Ish-
Bosheth, Saul's son, and Mephibosheth, Saul's grandson,
survived (2 Sam. 2:8-12; 3:14-15; 4:1-8; 9:1-13). What the
verse is telling us is that all the members of Saul's family who
died that day fell side by side fighting a common enemy.
Whatever differences in the past had caused Saul and his sons
to quarrel were set aside when it came to this last battle against
the Philistines. They stood together, a father and his sons.
David noted that loyalty when he said of Saul and Jonathan,
'... and in death they were not parted' (2 Sam. 1:23).

Saul was honoured as a *king*, for he died leading his people
into battle against the historic enemies of the Lord (10:1-3).
His soldiers were fiercely loyal to him, just as David had been
on the two occasions when the opportunity presented itself to
kill Saul, but he refused to do so (see 1 Sam. 24; 26). When
Saul asked his armour-bearer to kill him before the Philistines
captured him, the armour-bearer could not bring himself to do

the deed. Later, when the news of Saul's death spread (10:9-10), the men of Jabesh Gilead came to show their regard for Saul in a very special way (10:11-12).

The men of Jabesh Gilead had a special reason to be thankful to Saul. One of his first actions as king had been to rouse the Israelites to come to the aid of this isolated town when it had come under attack from the Ammonites (see 1 Sam. 11). That had been forty years earlier, but still the men of this town had an enduring loyalty to the king who had protected them from destruction. They showed their loyalty by a daring night-time raid to return the bodies of Saul and his sons to Israel for a decent burial (10:11-12).

Even David, who had been so fiercely and so wrongly persecuted by Saul, showed him respect in his death, although that is not recorded in this chapter. In 2 Samuel 1:14-16 we read how he dismissed the attempts of the young man who tried to curry favour with him by pretending that he had killed Saul. David asked him, 'Why were you not afraid to lift your hand to destroy the Lord's anointed?' (2 Sam. 1:14). David also composed a lament for Saul and his son Jonathan (2 Sam. 1:17-27).

The important lesson to be drawn from all these incidents was summarized by the apostle Paul in Romans 13:7: 'Give everyone what you owe him: if you owe taxes, pay taxes; if revenue, then revenue; if respect, then respect; if honour, then honour.' We are not simply to honour those we like, or those who may be kind to us, but all whom God has placed in positions of authority or dignity. Paul put that principle into practice on one very trying occasion when he was appearing before the Jewish ruling body, the Sanhedrin. When the presiding high priest ordered that Paul be struck unlawfully the apostle burst out in indignation, but when he realized to whom he had spoken he checked himself, saying, 'Brothers, I did not realize that he was the high priest; for it is written:

"Do not speak evil about the ruler of your people"' (Acts 23:3,5).

Those who have authority over us may not always be good, or their actions right. Yet, whether they are government officials, law enforcement officers, parents, or elders within the church, we owe them the respect that is due to those who hold their office.

The disgrace Saul suffered in his death

This was a dark day in the history of Israel. It was a day of *personal tragedy*. For many years Saul had been living in open defiance of God, stumbling along from one disaster to another. Because of his sin he found that God was no longer helping him as in the early days of his reign. Saul's nadir came when he knew that military defeat was looming and he asked for a medium to summon up the spirit of the dead prophet Samuel for advice (10:13; 1 Sam. 28). What Saul learned was that the Lord had forsaken him and that inevitable disaster was the result. Saul's military acumen deserted him and in panic he engaged the Philistines on the flat plain at the top of Mount Gilboa. This was to the great disadvantage of his armies because his Philistine opponents were able to use their superior chariots with devastating effect. Saul saw his armies routed and ended the day by committing suicide.

Suicide is always a great personal tragedy. It is a sinful breach of the sixth commandment, which, according to the application given in the *Westminster Shorter Catechism*, forbids 'the taking away of our own life, or the life of our neighbour unjustly, or whatsoever tendeth thereunto' (see Exod. 20:13; Acts 16:28). Here Saul sought to escape from a terrible disaster by fleeing into the righteous judgement of the God he had rejected.

That day was also a day of *family tragedy*, for on that day the best of Saul's family were wiped out (10:2,6). As we have already seen, there were survivors, but never again would the house of Saul be an influence in the land. A few malcontents would continue to hanker after the old days, but no standard-bearer would arise to give unity and coherence to their cause. They would be like the Jacobites who continued to support the royal house of Stuart after it lost the throne of England and Scotland in 1714. They failed to realize the hopelessness of their cause. So too the cause of Saul's house had been brought to nothing by the judgement of God upon sinful behaviour.

There were even wider repercussions from the events of that day, for it was a day of *national disaster*. We read that the Philistines occupied the towns of the valley beyond Mount Gilboa in the Jezreel valley (10:7). These were towns that Saul had captured after years of campaigning against the Philistines, yet they were lost in a single day. That day the gains of Saul's reign slipped through his dying fingers, and with them went the homes and livelihoods of many of his subjects. We can try to imagine the misery of families left fatherless and turned into homeless refugees.

This is a graphic demonstration of the misery caused to his people and the dishonour done to God by the failings of the king. How the Philistines gloated in their hour of triumph! (10:8-10). They exulted over Saul's humiliation in the temples of their false gods. Now that they had defeated the Lord's anointed they thought that they had broken the power of Jehovah, the God of Israel. Where previously David had cut off Goliath's head (1 Sam. 17:51), now the Philistines cut off Saul's head; and where their god Dagon had fallen before the ark of the covenant, breaking off its head in the process (1 Sam. 5:3-4), now Saul's head was impaled. The conflict on Mount Gilboa was spiritual in nature; it was a battle between God's enemies and God's people. So when it became clear that

God's enemies had won, it was with a devilish glee that the Philistines proclaimed **'the news'** of their victory **'among their idols and their people'**.

Saul's reign had begun with so much promise. He was one of the most outstanding young men of his generation; physically he was head and shoulders above those around him and as a military leader he turned the tide in the wars against the Philistines. Some were beginning to ask if this king could possibly be the promised deliverer of God's people. The answer was a resounding 'No!' For all his gifts, Saul lacked the quality that matters most in God's service: he was not wholehearted in serving the Lord, and for that reason he failed on the battlefield. This failure, like that of many others who profess to serve the Lord, was merely the outward manifestation of an inward and spiritual failure. Saul is a negative image of righteousness, showing what the Lord's anointed *will not* be like and demonstrating how terrible are the consequences of unfaithfulness.

The unfaithfulness that brought about Saul's death

In spite of all the respect that was paid to the King of Israel at his death, the judgement of God upon his life is recorded for us in 10:13-14. It is possible to have the praise of men heaped on us in this world, but that will pass away very quickly and have little lasting value if our hearts are not right with God. It is a sobering thought to realize that it is possible for us to receive much that is beneficial from unspiritual people and to owe a debt of gratitude to men and women who will come under everlasting condemnation. In spite of all that has been said about Saul, he was still a sinner.

This fact is summed up in verse 13, where we read that **'He was unfaithful to the Lord; he did not keep the word of the**

Lord.' On several occasions God spoke to Saul giving very clear guidance through Samuel the prophet. While Saul was waiting at Gilgal to fight the Philistines he could wait no longer for Samuel to come to offer sacrifices to God, so he offered them himself, and was rebuked by Samuel: 'You acted foolishly... You have not kept the command the Lord your God gave you; if you had, he would have established your kingdom over Israel for all time' (1 Sam. 13:13).

On another occasion Saul was asked to punish the Amalekites by slaughtering the whole nation and all their livestock (1 Sam. 15). Instead of carrying out God's commission Saul spared the king of the Amalekites and the best of the livestock. Samuel's rebuke was perceptive and pointed to the very nature of Saul's sinfulness. If he was willing to play fast and loose with God's commands, heeding some and ignoring others, he was in reality placing himself above God's rule and acting as if he did not need God at all. 'Rebellion', said Samuel, 'is like the sin of divination, and arrogance like the evil of idolatry' (1 Sam. 15:23), for both reject the supremacy of the Lord as the only true God, reducing him to the level of any other spiritual power to which men might turn in time of need. It comes therefore as no surprise that Saul continued his descent into evil to the point where he consulted a medium before the battle of Mount Gilboa. In 10:13 that incident is cited as the crowning symbol of Saul's unfaithfulness, and in modern culture the increasing interest in the occult is a sign that men and women have turned their backs on the true God and his word of truth — the Bible.

This is the very definition of unfaithfulness — despising what God has been pleased to reveal to us in his Word. When God gives us his Word it is to show us how to order our lives according to what is good. He expects us to seek out his Word and then to obey it. Saul did neither. Not only did he **'not enquire of the Lord'**, but he went out of his way to consult a medium for guidance (10:13,14; cf. 1 Sam. 28). This was expressly *forbidden* (Exod. 22:18; Lev. 19:26,31; Deut. 18:10-11). As a result of Saul's unfaithful behaviour, **'The Lord put him to death and turned the kingdom over to David son of Jesse'** (10:14). This illustrates a lesson the Chronicler is eager to teach God's people — that sinners will suffer immediate retribution for their own unfaithfulness.

The only antidote for unfaithfulness is keeping the Word of God close to our hearts — enquiring from within its pages what God would have us do in every situation we face. When there are decisions to be made, when temptation presses upon us, when our consciences are pricked, or when God shows us that there must be changes in our lives, then we must enquire of the Lord for guidance. That guidance he gives in his Word. In Psalm 119:11-12 the psalmist teaches us about the life of faithfulness:

> I have hidden your word in my heart
> that I might not sin against you.
> Praise be to you, O Lord;
> teach me your decrees.

7.
Loyalty to the king

Please read 1 Chronicles 11:1-25

The death of Saul left a great void at the centre of a badly shaken nation. The old enemy, the Philistines, had penetrated deep into Israelite territory and many Israelites had been driven from their homes. The historic tribal divisions in Israel had been exacerbated by Saul's paranoid behaviour, so that when he died a civil war broke out between the Benjamites and the other tribes which supported David. In his lifetime Saul had alienated even those who had been loyal supporters and as a result David, one of his leading generals, had become the fugitive leader of an armed band of outlaws.

The people of Israel needed to be united if they were to be liberated from enemy occupation. The task was a daunting one for any man. Any prospective successor to Saul would have asked the question that Paul the apostle was to ask many years later: 'Who is equal to such a task?' (2 Cor. 2:16). Certainly anyone facing this challenge in his own strength would have been crushed by the task. Only the man of God's appointing, going forward as the Lord's anointed, could face the challenges that awaited Saul's successor.

That man was David, the son of Jesse, whose family has already been singled out by our historian for special mention (3:1-24). Loyalty to the throne of David is of great importance to the Chronicler and is a sign of faithfulness to God himself.

Very briefly, David's seven-year reign at Hebron is mentioned in 11:1,3 but the reason why David spent those seven years in Hebron — and the civil war that raged during them — is not described in anything like the detail that we find in 2 Samuel 2-4. This is not because the writer wants to gloss over an embarrassing episode, but because he wishes to focus our attention on a theme that is very dear to his heart — and that is the unity of God's people as they submit to the reign of the Lord's anointed. David and his house had been appointed to rule over Israel, and in the Chronicler's eyes the reigns of David and Solomon his son were the golden age of Israel's history. This chapter describes how all Israel expressed their loyalty to David and united under his rule.

David's credentials (11:1-3)

When an ambassador arrives to represent his country to the government of another nation he must show his credentials before he can take up his office. He must provide evidence that he has been properly appointed to do the work that lies ahead of him. In this chapter David's credentials to reign as king are presented. It is not David himself who presents them (he has, after all, already been ruling as king for seven years in Hebron) but the people of all the tribes who come and ask him to rule over them. They show why he ought to be king, pointing to the Lord's blessing that has marked him out to be the ruler of Israel.

The blessing of God had attended David's leadership in Israel for many years, even during the reign of Saul (11:2). After killing the Philistine giant Goliath (1 Sam. 17), David rose through the ranks of Saul's army (1 Sam. 18:5). When his military genius outshone Saul's achievements the king was provoked to murderous jealousy. On hearing the women singing, 'Saul has slain his thousands, and David his tens of thousands' (1 Sam. 18:6-7), Saul resolved to kill David.

David rose to prominence in Saul's army because the Lord was with him. It soon became clear to everyone that he was no ordinary soldier, but a man uniquely blessed by God and prepared for a great task ahead (11:2). As the people saw that Saul had turned away from the Lord and had forfeited his blessing, it became increasingly clear that David enjoyed the blessing of God's presence in all that he did. While Saul's rule brought disaster to Israel, David's leadership brought them great blessing. Such a man must surely be the Lord's anointed!

We read in 1 Samuel 16 how the prophet Samuel was sent to anoint David to take Saul's place. When Samuel arrived at the home of Jesse the Bethlehemite the man of God's choosing was not Eliab, or Abinadab, or any of the sturdy warriors among David's brothers, but David the shepherd lad. The daily routine of a shepherd out in the wilderness had been God's training for the man who would lead his people. When David went out to fight against the giant Goliath he described how his background was such an excellent training for his life's work (1 Sam. 17:34-37). So when the people of Israel came to make David their king they quoted the Lord's commission: **'And the Lord your God said to you, "You will shepherd my people Israel, and you will become their ruler"'** (11:2).

Here is an interesting combination of qualities in David's role. He was appointed to a position of prominence as a 'ruler' over God's people. The Hebrew word is *nagid* and it derives from the verb meaning 'to be in front', or in a position of prominence, and it means 'a prince', or 'ruler'. It was used in the Old Testament of those who gave leadership in national life and was often associated with royal dignity.

As well as enjoying a position of honour, David was appointed to a role that carried a heavy burden of responsibility, for he was to be a shepherd king. Significantly, Paul prescribed a similar balance of honour and responsibility for those who serve as elders in the New Testament church (1 Tim. 3:1; 5:17). In keeping with the nature of God's commission to David, which the people quote with enthusiasm, the verbal (active participle) form is used: 'You will shepherd my people' (11:2). The word is *roeh*, which is the standard Old Testament word for 'shepherd'. This derives from the verb *raah* ('to feed'), for the shepherd was one who fed and cared for the flock entrusted to his care. In Psalm 23 there is an excellent description of the attentive care which a good shepherd gave to his flock — leading, feeding, restoring, guiding and protecting.

Another feature of the typical Eastern shepherd calls for comment at this juncture. Often the shepherd did not himself own the sheep entrusted to his care, but was employed, perhaps by several sheep-owners, to take care of their sheep. The shepherd was always accountable to the owners for his care of their sheep. Twice the phrase 'my people Israel' is attributed to God to remind David that this is precisely his status as shepherd and ruler over Israel: 'You shall shepherd my people Israel, and be ruler over my people Israel' (11:2, NKJV). God is Israel's Shepherd (see Ps. 80:1; Gen. 49:24) and David himself was to acknowledge that 'The Lord is my shepherd' (Ps. 23:1). David was not an autocrat, but a man dependent upon, and accountable to, God. Only because the Lord had delivered him from danger (1 Sam. 17:37) and helped him to perform the duties that had been delegated to him was David able to bear the responsibilities and enjoy the honour that came with his royal position.

David came to symbolize the ideal of the royal shepherd in Israel:

He chose David his servant
  and took him from the sheep pens;
from tending the sheep he brought him
  to be the shepherd of his people Jacob,
  of Israel his inheritance.
And David shepherded them with integrity of heart;
  with skilful hands he led them

(Ps. 78:70-72).

Unfortunately the pattern of leadership set by David was not followed by all those who came after him. A frequent lament of the prophets was that Israel was led by men who had no pastoral concern for the people (see Isa. 56:11; Ezek. 34:1-10; Zech. 11:4-17).

Although the people of Israel were given the promise that a truly great shepherd would rule over them (Ezek. 34:11-16,20-24), this promise was not realized until the Lord Jesus presented himself as the Shepherd who 'lays down his life for the sheep' (John 10:11; cf. Luke 15:3-7; 1 Peter 5:4). His sacrificial love and desire to care for the needs of his people are set before those who serve as leaders in the church today as the perfect model (John 21:15-17; Acts 20:28; 1 Peter 5:1-3).

On the day that Samuel sought out David to take the place of King Saul he anointed David to be king over God's people. So when David went up, against Goliath and against the Philistines, it was as the Lord's anointed Messiah that he went. Anointing is one of the most important and symbolic actions in the Old Testament. It is a sign of God's blessing coming down on the heads of his people, bringing renewal of strength and life (see Ps. 133). It is a symbol of the ministry of the Holy Spirit, who stirs up and strengthens the hearts of God's people to do his work. It was because he was the Lord's anointed that David was such a mighty and victorious king, able to present his credentials and command the loyalty and respect due to the king of all Israel.

The title of Messiah, however, properly belongs to an even more exalted King. Psalm 2:2 speaks of a Messiah whom God has made his King over all the earth and who will establish his rule over all, whether they are worshippers or enemies. This Messiah, the Lord Jesus Christ, presents his credentials to us in the gospel. The Gospels tell us of his mighty works (John 9:33; 14:11), his atoning death and his victorious resurrection. He is worthy of our loyalty and his gospel is worthy of our trust. In 1784 Andrew Fuller wrote a book entitled *The Gospel Worthy of all Acceptation.* Because of who Christ is, his gospel is worthy of our total trust and acceptance (1 Tim. 1:15). His credentials are seen in his perfect life and saving work, and they demand our loyalty and submission.

David's headquarters (11:4-9)

Although it is hard to put a precise date on the events in these verses, it would seem that they took place shortly after all the tribes of Israel united around David's rule. It is a sign of just how precarious David's kingdom was at this stage that Jerusalem (referred to in 11:4 by its Canaanite name, 'Jebus') was still in the hands of the Jebusites. These were Canaanite inhabitants of the promised land who had never been properly subdued when Joshua led the people into the land (see Josh. 13:1). When Israel was weakened through internal divisions or hostile invaders these enemies reasserted themselves and threatened the security of the Israelite nation.

Within this mountain stronghold in the very heart of Israel's territory God's enemies were entrenched and defiant. Their boast is recorded in verse 5: **'You will not get in here.'** The account of this incident in 2 Samuel 5:6 shows how arrogant they had become in their contempt for God's people: 'Even the blind and the lame can ward you off.' Boastful words like these only served to provoke David to action, so he gave the command: **'Whoever leads the attack on the Jebusites will become commander-in-chief'** (11:6). We can hear an echo of the righteous anger that had caused David to ask about the Philistine giant Goliath, 'Who is this uncircumcised Philistine that he should defy the armies of the living God?' (1 Sam. 17:26).

David knew that he was not fighting on his own, for the Lord was with him (11:9) and gave him the victory over the Jebusites. That day one of David's captains, Joab the son of Zeruiah, who was also his nephew, captured the fortress that became known as **'the City of David'** (11:5,7). Jerusalem became not just the seat, but also the symbol, of his monarchy over all Israel. When David captured Jerusalem there were changes to be made. He took up residence there, so the city had to be rebuilt as a capital fit to be the home of God's anointed king. Joab took responsibility for part of this work and in 11:8 we read that he **'restored the rest of the city'**. Literally, he 'revived' or 'brought life' to the city.

In the town where I live there is an organization called the Regeneration Trust which seeks to refurbish commercial premises and stimulate economic activity. The sort of new life that David sought to bring to Jerusalem was more significant even than commercial activity, for he wanted to make Jerusalem the spiritual capital of his kingdom. Starting as a stronghold of God's enemies, it was to become a place of true worship and spiritual life.

How sad it is when we see the Lord's enemies entrenched in positions of influence over people's lives, in our national life and, on occasions, even within the church! The problem is that the hearts of men have become a stronghold for the Evil One, who openly defies the authority of the Lord Jesus Christ.

Entrenched in his stronghold within the hearts of fallen men and women, Satan is deceitful and defiant. What David did to the Jebusite forces in the mountain stronghold of Jerusalem is what the grace of God must do in our hearts if we are to become his servants and enjoy his salvation. Our Lord bore testimony to our need for a mighty act of regeneration that will bring new life into our souls and transform them from bastions of evil into strongholds of righteousness when he told Nicodemus, 'I tell you the truth, no one can see the kingdom of God unless he is born again' (John 3:3). This is a sovereign, transforming work of the Holy Spirit that destroys for ever the dominance of the Evil One and silences his boasts by producing renewed lives that glorify our Saviour.

David's warriors (11:10-25)

These verses list the names of those who stood by David and showed their loyalty to him. A simple list of names of men from a wide variety of backgrounds is given in 11:26-47, and this will be considered in the next chapter. The list in verses 10-25 is made all the more interesting by the touches of personal detail that tell us about the characters of the men who served David and how they demonstrated their loyalty.

Many of the men listed in these verses had been with David during his time as a fugitive from King Saul. They had risked their lives to stand beside him, so they were not fair-weather friends. They were hardy men, who had survived in the harshest of wilderness conditions. They were a band of comrades, loyal to each other and to their commander. Some, of course, were closer to David than others. There was a special group of strong and brave men known as **'the Thirty'** (11:25). Just as our Lord had some disciples with whom he was particularly intimate, so David was served by **'the three mighty men'** (11:12).

These men demonstrated their loyalty to David with an extraordinary zeal. They performed almost superhuman acts of bravery and stamina. Eleazar son of Dodai the Ahohite stood alone against a whole party of Philistines and was exposed to attack from all sides in the middle of a barley field (11:13-14). Benaiah son of Jehoida faced the fury of man and beast, wrenching a spear out of the hand of an Egyptian and killing him with his own spear, and going down into a pit on a snowy day (no easy task in itself) to face a lion (11:22-23).

The special relationship between David and his men is illustrated by the incident described in 11:15-19. On this occasion David expressed a longing that he might drink water from the well in his home town of Bethlehem (11:17). If his concern had been merely to satisfy his physical thirst, then water from any well would have sufficed (and exposed his men to less risk!), but our historian sets David's longing against the background of the political situation described in 11:16: **'The Philistine garrison was at Bethlehem.'** This was a source of shame and grief to the Bethlehemites (amongst whom David numbered himself) and an occasion of danger to David's followers who went to seek the water.

Their zeal is like the bravery of Francis Drake and the small party of English sailors who sailed into Cadiz harbour to destroy ships and stores that were being prepared for the Spanish Armada's assault on England the following year. Drake referred to this audacious strike as 'singeing the King of Spain's beard'. The bravery — almost to the point of foolhardiness — of Drake and his companions has become a part of English folklore. The incident recorded in these verses displays a similar mixture of reckless bravery, patriotism and, above all, a devotion to their leader. Facing great danger, these men broke through the Philistine lines to bring water back to David (11:18).

David's response to their action showed that he appreciated the risks that his followers had taken. The water was more precious to him than other water — even from the well in Bethlehem — because men had risked their lives to bring it. It was as precious as lifeblood! In a very public way, David showed how much this meant to him, for he poured the water out onto the ground as an offering and said, **'Should I drink the blood of these men who went at the risk of their lives?'** (11:19). In this way David showed his gratitude to God for such loyal supporters. His public pouring out of the water was an act of worship and thanksgiving to God. A willing people is a gift from God and in Psalm 110:3 David anticipated a band of willing followers who would place themselves at the service of the divine Messiah:

> Your troops will be willing
>   on your day of battle.
> Arrayed in holy majesty,
>   from the womb of the dawn
>   you will receive the dew of your youth.

The true nature of the zeal of David's followers is described in 11:10: **'They, together with all Israel, gave his** [i.e., David's] **kingship strong support to extend it over the whole land, as the Lord had promised.'** They took delight in God's promises and sought to establish the kingdom of the one that the Lord had anointed. As Christian believers serving the mighty Lord of heaven, who has risen from the grave to conquer every enemy, including death itself, our zeal and willingness to face hardship in his service ought to surpass that of men like Eleazar son of Dodai and Benaiah son of Jehoiada. Does it? Are we loyal servants of the King of kings?

8.
God's army

Please read 1 Chronicles 11:26 - 12:40

Christians cannot agree with the maxim of the Chinese Communist leader Mao Tse Tung that 'Power grows out of the barrel of a gun.' The Bible teaches us that political leaders exercise their rule by the appointment of God, and no amount of military might can frustrate his plans to raise up one or bring down another. We do, however, recognize that lawful governments must use some measure of force (or, as Paul put it in Romans 13:4, they 'bear the sword') to enforce their authority. We saw that illustrated in the first part of chapter 11, where David was recognized as the lawful King of Israel; now we consider the army of supporters which, humanly speaking, became his power base.

An army is never an easy organization to govern. It brings together aggressive and restless men from a wide variety of backgrounds with so much energy that could be put to destructive, as well as constructive, uses. These men need to be fed, watered, disciplined and given useful work to do; otherwise they can become a rabble rather than an army. David faced many of the problems that generals in modern armies face, but he had one unique advantage, for this was not an ordinary army. David's army had been gathered for the purpose of putting the Lord's anointed onto the throne of Israel. For that reason it was likened to **'the army of God'** (12:22).

The period covered by this chapter stretches back to David's 'wilderness years', when it had become obvious, not just that Saul had deserted the Lord, but that the Lord had rejected Saul and had anointed another to take his place of leadership. During part of that time David had his headquarters at Ziklag (12:1) and later he found sanctuary in the territory of the Philistines (12:19-22). Throughout those years a steady stream of supporters came to give their loyalty to David and they are mentioned in 12:1-22. In 12:23-40 and 11:26-47, the Chronicler summarizes by describing the army that David had amassed by the time that the whole nation of Israel acknowledged him as their king at Hebron.

As we study this passage there are several lessons we can learn about God's army today — the church. The Lord Jesus Christ is the anointed Messiah and the King of kings. His army is a band of believing people who are devoted to him and dedicated to championing his kingly rights. What sort of a body, therefore, ought his church to be? Let us notice several features of David's army that will help us to answer that question.

Diversity

Many different types of people were brought together to form this army. In 12:1-22 we read how representatives of the different tribal groups in Israel rallied around David. Israel had been a very divided nation in which men were more loyal to their tribe than to the nation. Yet the passage shows that all Israel united behind David.

First of all, there were the kinsmen of Saul from the tribe of Benjamin (12:1-7). Hard as it might have been for this group to accept, they recognized that Saul had sinned and that Benjamin had forfeited the prerogative of the crown. Other

Benjamites came and their pledge of loyalty is recorded in 12:16-18.

From the tribe of Gad (one of the lesser tribes which occupied territory on the eastern side of the Jordan) came a band of supporters (12:8-15). The physical obstacles that they had to cross on their way to reach him (12:15) and their great bravery in battle (12:14) show us the depth of their commitment to David.

In 12:19 we also read of men coming to David from the tribe of Manasseh. As we have seen already, Manasseh represented what later became known as the northern kingdom of Israel. Although the split between north and south only manifested itself as partition into two kingdoms during the reign of Rehoboam, the son of Solomon, the fault line had existed for many generations. There seems to have been a large measure of suspicion and jealousy between the smaller tribes and the much larger tribe of Judah. The coming together of the tribes in this chapter shows how the Lord's anointed overcame petty prejudices and divisions so that his people might live as one nation.

Even foreigners were gathered into the nation of Israel to serve in the Lord's army (11:39,41). We note the mention of Uriah the Hittite, who served David with great loyalty in the battlefield, even though his loyalty was so poorly rewarded (see 2 Sam. 11:6-24).

We also notice that everyone had a distinctive contribution to make to God's army, for many different types of people are specifically mentioned. In any country whose security is threatened by hostile neighbours, martial skills such as strength and courage would be of great importance. Naturally the Chronicler notes such skills: for example, the relations of Saul **'were able to shoot arrows or to sling stones right-handed or left-handed'** (12:2), and it was said of the men of Gad that **'The least was a match for a hundred, and the greatest for a thousand'** (12:14; cf. 12:8,30,33).

There were other contributions just as worthy of record. The great general Napoleon knew that 'An army marches on its stomach' and would have appreciated the gifts of the soldiers' families and of the men of Issachar, Zebulun and Naphtali who supplied food and drink for the fighting men (12:39-40). This army enjoyed the support of the people, morale was high — **'There was joy in Israel'** — and all this enhanced its effectiveness as a military force.

The men of Issachar are described as men **'who understood the times and knew what Israel should do'** (12:32). This is not, as has been suggested, a reference to the Persian practice of astrology (as in Esther 1:13). Instead it was the gift of insight into the revealed will of God and the capacity to apply that truth to the times in which they lived. Such figures have had great influence for good in the church throughout the ages. We can think of men like C. H. Spurgeon, Francis Schaeffer and Martyn Lloyd-Jones in more recent times and we should pray that God would raise up such prophetic figures in our own day.

In the church there will always be a great variety of people, with different temperaments, interests and gifts. That is because God equips his servants for different areas and levels of service. The apostle Paul describes the church as a body with many different organs (1 Cor. 12:14-20). Because this is how the Holy Spirit has distributed gifts amongst God's people our biblical doctrine of the church teaches us to expect this and to regard it as a blessing. Too often people expect the body of believers to be a group of individuals just like themselves, and consequently find diversity an irritant. Apart from the sinfulness of this attitude, it blinds the church to the blessings God bestows upon the body of his people by bringing together a diverse array of skills and strengths.

Unity

The mention of the array of tribal groups in this passage emphasizes another of the themes that threads its way through the history of Chronicles — that all Israel came to support David. We have considered the diversity of the individuals who came to support him, but although they were very different in many ways they were all united around King David.

The New Testament emphasizes the unity of the church around David's greatest descendant, the Lord Jesus. The church is a body with many different parts, but it is the head who gives life, unity and direction to all the lesser limbs (Eph. 1:22; 4:15; 5:23). Christ is described as 'the Head, from whom the whole body, supported and held together by its ligaments and sinews, grows as God causes it to grow' (Col. 2:19).

A most important expression of that unity is the service that each part of the body gives to Christ. We note that each member of this army **'came to help David'** (12:22). It is the calling of each believer to dedicate himself and his gifts to his Saviour. As well as expressing the unity of God's people, the acts of service mentioned in this chapter had the effect of cementing that unity. It is important to notice the frequent use of the word 'help' in this passage (12:1,17-19,21-22,33). By their coming and their service these helpers entered into a special relationship with the king. They gave themselves wholeheartedly to the very important work of establishing God's kingdom on earth, and in so doing found themselves bound together in greater harmony with the king and with each other. At the centre of all this activity was David, behind whose kingdom all these people were united: **'The Israelites were ... of one mind to make David king'** (12:38). In serving the king their unity as a nation was strengthened.

For this reason it is such an awful thing to see professing Christians shirk from their responsibilities as members of the church. This has the effect of paralysing the body of Christ, when as a result of inactivity important limbs or organs are simply not functioning as God intended them. Not all of us can preach or teach a class, but we can all pray, we can all tithe and we can all be 'doorkeepers in the house of God' (see Ps. 84:10). What a difference it would make to the life of the church and the honour of Christ if all of God's people were united in loving service of the Saviour!

Loyalty

There was unity in the work of the kingdom because there was an intense personal loyalty to the Lord's anointed. The people were wholeheartedly behind their king and were devoted to him (12:38). The Chronicler noted this because David had good reason to suspect the loyalty of some of the men who came to him — in particular Saul's relations from the tribe of Benjamin. Were they, perhaps, jealous that the crown had passed to another family and another tribe? Would they betray him?

These were questions that David asked himself as he proceeded with caution: **'David went out to meet them and said to them, "If you have come to me in peace, to help me, I am ready to have you unite with me. But if you have come to betray me to my enemies when my hands are free from violence, may the God of our fathers see it and judge you"'** (12:17). David was cautious until his fears were overcome by the answer Amasai gave to his questions:

We are yours, O David!
We are with you, O son of Jesse!

> **Success, success to you,**
> **and success to those who help you,**
> **for your God will help you**
>
> (12:18).

The men of Zebulun also typify this same spirit. They helped David **'with undivided loyalty'** (12:33). Literally the phrase means that they served God, 'not with one heart and then another'. The translation of the Authorized Version is a good one: 'They were not of double heart.' They did not have two hearts pulling in different directions — one heart loyal to David, and the other heart not so sure.

Such confusion among God's people can only ever be dangerous. For this reason Gideon sent the bulk of his army home before he fought against the Midianites (Judg. 7:3). These were men who were not sure whether they wanted to stay and fight or return to their families, so he fought the Midianites with a greatly reduced fighting force, but the men who went into battle with him were dedicated to the Lord.

Jesus told his disciples that they could not serve two masters, but would serve either God or mammon (Luke 16:13). We cannot serve Christ and flirt with the world, for one or the other will command our ultimate loyalty. James even went so far as to say that the man whose loyalty is divided 'should not think he will receive anything from the Lord; he is a double-minded man, unstable in all he does' (James 1:7-8). This is the most common cause of failure in the Christian life and it arises when our loyalty to Christ is compromised by loyalty to the world. Our only remedy is daily commitment of ourselves to serve the Lord, and him only. In all things he must have the pre-eminence in our lives (see Col. 1:18).

The work of the Holy Spirit

In conclusion let us look at one feature which explains much that we have learned about this army. In 12:18 we read about the working of the Holy Spirit. As a result of his prompting Amasai, a member of the tribe of Benjamin, declared his loyalty to the house of David. What could have brought about such an amazing transformation? Nothing but a mighty work of the Holy Spirit of God. Amasai became his spokesman, and displayed the great transformation that had taken place in his life and in the lives of many others besides.

It is the work of God's Holy Spirit amongst his people that makes them a mighty army. In his vision of the valley of dry bones Ezekiel saw how the Spirit of God turned the dry bones into a living army. The dry bones were gathered together and clothed with flesh and the breath of life came into them when Ezekiel prophesied as God commanded him and the breath of God went forth (Ezek. 37:9-10). Without this movement of God's Spirit there is neither life nor strength, nor a people to serve him. Two features of his ministry are illustrated with especial clarity in this verse.

1. A great transformation takes place in the lives of God's servants

This is illustrated by a very significant phrase in 12:18, where we are told that **'The Spirit came upon Amasai.'** The Hebrew phrase is that 'The Spirit clothed himself with Amasai', so that Amasai became like a glove-puppet in the hands of the sovereign Spirit of grace. It is not that Amasai lost anything of his personality, but rather that he gained a new driving force. Amasai still spoke and acted in all that happened, but the controlling influence was no longer his sinful and rebellious nature. Instead it was the grace of God now alive in his soul. This gracious influence is also described in Colossians 1:27 and 2 Peter 1:3-4.

This transforming work of grace takes place in the life of every person who will go to be with Christ in heaven, because God's people must be fitted for heaven. We should never underestimate the changes that God works in the lives of his people to save them, for sometimes the work of transformation can be painful. Samuel Rutherford wrote to one of his friends, 'Alas, it is neither easy nor ordinary to believe and be saved!' The work of God turns us inside out, purges sinful behaviour, and transforms us from being slaves of sinful and selfish pursuits to being instruments of righteousness dedicated to Christ. To him we now say, 'We are yours... We are with you, O Son of Jesse!'

2. The loving declaration made by God's servants (12:18)

Matthew Henry comments on this verse: 'From these expressions of Amasai we may take instruction how to testify our affection and allegiance to the Lord Jesus.' We can also learn about the love that binds God's people together. Amasai's prayer for David is '*Shalom* to you' — 'May you enjoy the peace that only God can give' — and there is no better prayer that we can pray for anyone.

This loving loyalty is the evidence of the working of God's Spirit amongst his people. When Paul describes the fruit of the Spirit in Galatians 5:22-23, he first of all mentions 'love'. Thomas Chalmers connected the working of God's Spirit with 'the expulsive power of new affection'. This means that we show our new birth by demonstrating our love to Christ and his people in ways that can be seen. Without this all our professions of faith are an empty show (1 Cor. 13:1-3).

9.
Uzzah and the ark

Please read 1 Chronicles 13:1-14

The events of this chapter are a sad but important landmark in the history of David's reign. David began to turn his attention to reforming the religious life of the people of Israel, but his plans were overshadowed and delayed by the tragic death of Uzzah.

The ark of the covenant was a very important symbol in the religion of the Old Testament. It was a wooden box overlaid with gold, built according to instructions given to Moses in Exodus 25:10-22, stored in the most holy room in the tabernacle and later the temple. Inside the ark were the two tablets of stone on which the Ten Commandments had been engraved, and at various times a gold pot containing a sample of manna from the wilderness and Aaron's rod that blossomed were also kept in it (Heb. 9:4).

The ark symbolized the *presence* of God amongst his people, for his glory dwelt **'between the cherubim'**, and the *character* of God, for **'The ark ... is called by the Name'** (13:6) and it contained the law that is a transcript of God's holy character. As a token of the reverence due to God, the ark was not to be touched by sinful human hands. It is important to remember that the ark also symbolized the *mercy* of God, for its lid was also the mercy-seat on which the high priest sprinkled the blood of the sacrificial animal each year on the Day of Atonement to blot out the sins of the whole nation (see Lev. 16:1-34).

David sought to bring this symbol into his new capital city, Jerusalem, and place it at the centre of his kingdom. By this action David showed what sort of a king he wanted to be, for he was more than just a successful warlord in the nation of Israel. David was also a spiritual leader and the movement of the ark was an important new development in his reign.

David acknowledged his calling to serve God (13:1-4)

David wanted his people to realize that he was more than simply a military leader, concerned only with fighting battles, defeating enemies and building fortresses. He was pre-eminently a man of God, described as a man after God's own heart. He was 'the sweet psalmist of Israel' who, in the Psalter, has left us some of the most profoundly spiritual writings in the whole canon of Scripture. As a spiritual leader of his people he sought to lead them to a closer walk with the Lord who had given them every blessing.

In this passage we read how David gathered his people together to remind them of their obligation to God. He conferred with the leaders of Israel (13:1), then he gathered the whole nation and said, **'If it seems good to you and if it is the will of the Lord our God ... let us bring the ark of our God back to us'** (13:2-3). David was right to be cautious. Firstly, he did not want to rush into a project only to find that he had overlooked God's revealed will, so he sought the counsel of others. Then, secondly, he wanted to engage the whole nation in this project to restore true worship to Israel. He wanted all the people to share his enthusiasm for the Lord, so he involved them at an early stage and shared his plans with them.

Above all, he wanted to remind the people of the goodness and greatness of the God of Israel. They were under his authority and were answerable to him. They were to seek God's guidance to direct their lives and needed to be in a right relationship with him. They needed to come to God via the blood-sprinkled way that God had shown in his Word. God had ordered the construction of the ark as a visible symbol of his covenant with his people, and it was wrong that this symbol should be banished to obscurity. David showed his delight for God's truth by bringing the ark back to the centre of his kingdom in Jerusalem. He was also acknowledging that all his armies and victories and palaces were as nothing if he did not use the authority they gave him to direct his people to serve the God of the covenant.

This puts our earthly achievements in perspective. We can gain great success for ourselves, but surely the test by which our lives will be judged in eternity is how well we have used the gifts God gave us to glorify him. Our governments can give us ever higher standards of living, but if they do not exalt Christ, they are failures. Parents want to do the best they can for their children. They will give them presents, education and every opportunity within their grasp, but the best legacy any parent can leave his or her children is to train them in the knowledge of the Lord. This is the lesson we learn from David in these verses.

David remedied past forgetfulness of God (13:3-6)

During Saul's reign the ark had been ignored as a symbol of God's covenant with his people (13:3). Those forty long years had been a time of spiritual declension when God was neither sought nor honoured by the nation's king. Saul had made a promising start, but very soon he started to rely on his own instincts rather than on the guidance of God. As a result David inherited a spiritual wasteland, ruined by forty years of godless leadership. Notice, however, how David approached his task.

1. He acknowledged a degree of guilt

He did not shrug his shoulders and lay all the blame on Saul and a previous generation of national leaders. David and the men of his generation were part of the nation and they shared in the nation's guilt, as they confessed when he said, **'For we did not enquire of it** [the ark] **during the reign of Saul'** (13:3). This is how Nehemiah prayed when he mourned over the sins that resulted in the exile: 'I confess the sins we Israelites, including myself and my father's house, have committed against you. We have acted very wickedly towards you. We have not obeyed the commandments, decrees and laws you gave your servant Moses' (Neh. 1:6-7). Even when God's people have not personally committed those particular sins, they are affected by them by virtue of belonging to a sinful community — and ought to mourn over them before God.

We, in our time, ought to consider the sins of our nations — materialism, blasphemy, Sabbath-breaking, corruption — and realize that we cannot cut ourselves off from those around us who perpetrate them. Have we cried out against national wickedness? Have we sought to turn others from these sins? Or have we allowed the sins of our culture to influence us, even in our thinking? Reformation begins when the people of God look to themselves and mourn at the defilement of their own hearts (Matt. 5:4) and the widespread consequences.

2. He could not undo the sins of the past, but he could make sure that they were not compounded

As well as the sin of Saul, who ignored the ark, there were the sins of Hophni and Phinehas, who abused the ark. When facing the Philistine armies in battle they took the ark with them, thinking of it as some sort of magic charm which could be turned to their advantage. Instead of overcoming the Philistines with the aid of the ark, they lost it to the Philistines, and it was returned to Israel only after God visited the Philistine cities with a series of disasters (1 Sam. 4-6). Afraid of its power, the people of Israel had the ark kept at Kiriath Jearim and showed no concern to bring it up to the tabernacle at Shiloh, or to any other place where it would have prominence in national life (1 Sam. 6:20 - 7:1). So when David sought to bring the ark to Jerusalem it was to be found languishing in Kiriath Jearim, as it had been for many years (13:6).

This sinful record of disregard for the Lord and his covenant had scarred the spiritual life of Israel and it would take many years to repair the damage. There was a legacy of invasion, destruction, death and sacrilege. The faith of many in Israel had been weakened. David could not undo all of that damage immediately, but he remedied what he could. He brought the ark up to Jerusalem and showed due honour to this symbol of God's law and presence.

In our lives there will be sins that we can never remedy — words said that can never be taken back, actions that can never be undone, opportunities missed that can never be claimed. These are like water that has flowed under a bridge never to return. But there are things that we can do right now to remove an offence. These we ought to do immediately. We can make sure that past failures are not repeated and that duties we have neglected in the past are not still being neglected now.

David discovered the awesomeness of God (13:7-11)

These verses illustrate the fact that it is possible to act with good intentions and still fall into serious sin. David's intention in bringing the ark from Kiriath Jearim was to honour God by bringing the symbol of his presence to the heart of the kingdom. He wanted to show that the years of neglect under Saul had come to an end. But David forgot that when sinful men draw near to God they must come in the way that God has laid down in his Word.

God does not show his will for our lives simply by giving us intuitions in our heads. That is the assumption that many people make today as they seek to live the Christian life. Very often we hear people say that they did something, or followed some course of action, because they 'felt led' or because it 'seemed good' to them. These subjective feelings are never submitted to any serious examination at the bar of God's Word. It is simply taken for granted that the Holy Spirit must have put the idea into the person's thoughts.

David was a man after God's own heart, but he was still a sinner. He faced the very real danger of being waylaid by his own indwelling sin. He was also a finite man who could not possibly know everything there was to know about God, so he was to make up for his deficiencies by turning to God for guidance. In that era, before the canon of Scripture was completed, there were prophets who were able to give guidance from God, and even in those days there was the written Law to which God's people turned to discover how God would have them worship him.

God's Word tells us what God is like. He is not to be approached thoughtlessly or treated casually, but exactly as he has prescribed in Scripture. God had shown that the ark, which was the symbol of his presence, was not to be handled as an ordinary object might be. It was to be carried on poles by the

Levites (Exod. 25:12-15; Num. 4:15; 7:9; 1 Chron. 15:2). Yet in his enthusiasm David forgot these commands and omitted to consult God's Word for guidance. We might be impressed by the enthusiasm displayed as **'David and all the Israelites were celebrating with all their might before God'** (13:8). God, however, was not impressed, but angered by David's carelessness. The ark had been manhandled onto an ox-cart and was being transported in just the same way as it had been by the Philistines (13:7; cf. 1 Sam. 6:7-12).

God's anger was revealed when Uzzah (one of the sons of Abinadab, in whose house the ark had been kept since it was returned by the Philistines, 2 Sam. 3:6), reached out his hand to steady the ark when the oxen stumbled and it threatened to fall to the ground. Uzzah had done something that was strictly forbidden. He had showed a familiarity with holy things that no man was permitted to show and as a result, **'The Lord's anger burned against Uzzah, and he struck him down because he had put his hand on the ark'** (13:10). David too was at fault because he should never have allowed the ark to be transported as it had been — on a bullock cart! God's anger is explained further in 15:13: 'It was because ... the Levites did not bring it up the first time that the Lord our God broke out in anger.' For all David's enthusiasm, he was sincerely wrong and seriously misguided in his behaviour. He had not searched the Scriptures for his directions in serving God.

To some people God's wrath in this chapter may appear petty and vindictive. That is because we do not truly understand the nature of God's holiness. He does nothing without good reason and all his commands are governed by his righteousness. So when God issues a command there are compelling reasons that lie behind it. How the ark of the covenant was to be transported was not a trivial matter because God had taken the trouble to show that there was a way that was acceptable to him. Any other way was therefore not acceptable to God and it was not for his people to improve on God's laws. When we question the details of God's commands we question his goodness and wisdom. Similarly when we ignore God's instructions we treat him as one of the many false gods, one who must stand trial before the court of human judgement.

David was badly shaken by the death of Uzzah (13:11). That day he learned a very important lesson: the Word of the Lord was to be the rule that governed his life and especially his worship. Neither the good intentions of our hearts nor the example of others are the guiding lights that we ought to follow. The fact that the Philistines had moved the ark on an ox-cart and appeared to suffer no harm was not a guarantee that David could behave in the same way with impunity. The wicked only seem to escape punishment for their actions, but when we look towards 'their final destiny' (Ps. 73:17) we see a very different picture. In any case God expects a higher standard of obedience from those who have known his saving grace than from those who have not.

David forfeited God's blessing (13:12-14)

David's anger following Uzzah's death (13:11) very quickly turned into fear (13:12). This was not that reverent fear that all God's children are to show to their heavenly Father, but the servile fear of those who have seen the terror of the Lord and have turned away. As a result David abandoned his plan to bring the ark to Jerusalem. This was a very sad turn of events for the ark was the symbol, not just of God's holiness, but also of his mercy. The mercy-seat was the place where blood was sprinkled for the forgiveness of sins and atonement was secured. Yet the ark had brought tragedy to David's household and it seemed safer to put it away for the time being. The ark was left at the home of Obed-Edom the Gittite and David forfeited blessing as a result (13:13-14).

A very hard lesson was being taught to David through these events. He learned that indwelling, and often unconscious, sinfulness was still a very powerful reality in his heart. Often in his dealings with us God shows us what we are really like underneath the image we present to others, and that can be a painful discovery. It is the breaking down that comes before the building up, the godly sorrow that precedes godly joy. In David's case two unsavoury traits of character were exposed that day at Perez Uzzah.

1. Anger leading to resentment

When people suffer they sometimes direct their anger against God. They ask, 'Why has God made me suffer so? How can he be a good God? How can he expect me to trust in him now?' Such anger is a distraction from the real issue presented to us by tragic events like the death of Uzzah. There is not one of us in this world who is not a sinner and who does not deserve to suffer, both now and in eternity. By confronting us with this fact God warns us to seek his mercy now! He shows us that unless we repent of our sin, we shall all perish (Luke 13:5). Repentance, not resentment, is our only appropriate response when God chastises us.

2. Fear leading to retreat

Because of the terrible shock that he had received David sought to hide from God for a time, following the pattern of sinful behaviour that Adam and Eve had established just after the first sin in Genesis 3:8. David asked, **'How can I ever**

bring the ark of God to me?' and lodged it in the home of Obed-Edom rather than bring it to Jerusalem. This was, of course, an attempt to hide from the lessons that God was teaching David. Rather than turn to God, asking how he had gone astray and what God would have him to do, David set the ark aside and returned home. In this he was like the apostle Peter when he pleaded with his Lord, 'Go away from me, Lord; I am a sinful man!' (Luke 5:8), or the erstwhile disciples of Jesus who left him saying, 'This is a hard teaching. Who can accept it?' (John 6:60). As a result David forfeited blessing that could have been his. Instead of David enjoying the blessing that accompanies God's presence, that blessing was enjoyed by Obed-Edom and his family for three months (13:14). The cost of fear that led to retreat was forfeited blessing.

Still today some people forfeit blessing when they consider the holiness of God and say, 'I could never live the Christian life.' When God speaks to them in his gospel they retreat back to the world and to perdition rather than flee to the cross where sinners may be saved. When the gospel of the cross is preached Satan whispers in our ears to tell us of the cost, of the changes and the sacrifices we shall have to make. He urges us to turn away from God because his way of salvation is too hard. The devil points to an easier way — the way of retreat.

Our Lord Jesus openly admitted to his disciples that following him would mean learning some painful lessons and taking a difficult stand: 'In this world you will have trouble. But take heart! I have overcome the world' (John 16:33). It is as if our Lord tells us that when we follow him we shall come to our Perez Uzzah, but we must always remember the blessing that Obed-Edom enjoyed. This is the blessing that belongs to those who do not draw back but press on to serve the Lord faithfully.

10.
Following failure

Please read 1 Chronicles 14:1-17

The proprietor of a British newspaper in the 1930s was said to 'love the sin and hate the sinner' when scandal was reported by his newspaper. This fascination with sin for its own sake has become a distinguishing feature of the British tabloid press, and exploits a sinful trait in the human heart. A prurient interest in the sins of others can sometimes be a welcome distraction from the sins in our own lives and can even make us feel as if our sins are not so bad after all!

The inspired historians of the Bible are always refreshingly honest in the way they present the lives of the great figures of Israel's history. They admit the frailty of these men and at times even recount in detail the painful narrative of their sin and failure, but they never describe sin simply for its own sake. They never indulge our sinful curiosity about what is ugly and unbecoming. There is always a morally edifying purpose behind the narrative of God's salvation history.

The Chronicler continues his account of the life of King David in this chapter by showing how David moved on from his failure in chapter 13. In fact we cannot understand this chapter without referring back to the preceding chapter, nor ought we to consider the failure in chapter 13 without noting how David responded in chapter 14. Some commentators have suggested that we cannot be sure exactly when in David's reign the events of chapter 14 took place, but we shall make the working assumption that both the restoration of the ark and the Philistine raids came shortly after David was established as king in Jerusalem. The fact that the Chronicler interrupts the narrative of the ark's removal to Jerusalem with the account of the Philistine raids and David's response to them suggests that there is a significant chronological sequence in these chapters. David suffered because he failed to seek guidance from God before bringing the ark to Jerusalem, and in the very next chapter we find that David learned to seek God's guidance before going into battle. A very much wiser and godlier David finally brought the ark to Jerusalem in chapter 15.

The purpose of chapter 14 is to balance David's failure with a picture of his faithfulness. We see how David learned from his failure and pressed on.

David was blessed by God (14:1-7)

These verses put past failings in their proper perspective. We are shown that it is possible for a man of God to fail very badly and very publicly. Later on David would sin by committing adultery with Bathsheba and conniving at the murder of Uriah. Psalm 51 describes the painful consequences in David's life. He lost the joy of his salvation and felt cast out from God's presence (Ps. 51:11-12), but he never lost his *status* as a man of God.

As chapter 13 has already shown, David had sinned in his treatment of the ark, having it carried on an ox-cart rather than by the Levites, as God had commanded Moses. As a result Uzzah had touched the ark when he should not have done and had been struck down in an outburst of the Lord's holy anger.

David's rejoicing before the Lord was quickly transformed
into anger and fear and his plans to bring the ark to Jerusalem
were shelved and replaced by a sulky silence. A family was
bereft of a loved one and the king had lost face before his
people. Yet in spite of this very public humiliation and sadness
David's status as a man of God was unchanged. The grace of
God teaches us that, since we are not saved by our righteous
actions (Eph. 2:8), our failings cannot undermine our standing
before God. David is one of the greatest biblical examples of
this truth.

This truth is emphasized in a variety of ways in 14:1-7,
where the Chronicler goes out of his way to show just how
richly God blessed David. The blessings mentioned in this
section include the respect of his neighbour, Hiram king of
Tyre (14:1), gifts of building materials and workmen to build
a palace for him (14:1) and the expansion of his family to
include more wives, sons and daughters (14:3-7). Although
the Bible does not teach a simple linkage between material
prosperity and God's favour, it is a distinctive feature of the
book of Chronicles that lists of material gifts, military victories and growing families are used to indicate that an
individual enjoys God's favour. After all, God is the giver of
every good and perfect gift!

These gifts simply served to confirm God's testimony that
David had been anointed to lead Israel and deliver his people
from the contempt of their enemies. Verse 2 describes the
reassurance that God gave to his shaken servant through these
symbolic blessings, showing David that he was still the Lord's
anointed: **'David knew that the Lord had established him
as king over Israel and that his kingdom had been highly
exalted for the sake of his people Israel.'** David's reputation
was restored both at home and abroad (14:1,17) and God's
grace to sinners was demonstrated.

God's grace to his people never fails. We fail and bring chastisement on ourselves. In David's case Uzzah lay dead. We should never underestimate the pain and shame that our sin can bring upon ourselves and upon others, and most especially the dishonour it does to God. The Westminster divines expressed it as follows: 'Nevertheless they [that is, true believers] may, through the temptations of Satan and of the world, the prevalency of corruption in them, and the neglect of the means of their preservation, fall into grievous sins; and for a time continue therein: whereby they incur God's displeasure, and grieve his Holy Spirit; come to be deprived of some measure of their graces and comforts; have their hearts hardened, and their consciences wounded; hurt and scandalize others, and bring temporal judgements upon themselves' (*Westminster Confession of Faith*,17.3).

We should also remember that Satan will play upon the unpredictability of our consciences (Rom. 2:15) and will play down the constancy of God's mercy. We need to place our own failings and the failings of others in the perspective of God's restoring grace. 'They whom God hath accepted in his Beloved, effectually called and sanctified by his Spirit, can neither totally fall away from the state of grace; but shall certainly persevere therein to the end, and be eternally saved' (*Westminster Confession,* 17.1).

David was strengthened by God (14:8-12)

At times we look back on our past lives and say, 'If only...' We carry sorrow and regrets from past failings into the future. David must have experienced such regrets as he thought about the problems he had inherited from the time of his predecessor Saul as well as the new ones he had created for himself. At such times God's people do well to remember the biblical doctrine of providence. The Bible teaches us that God has foreordained whatsoever comes to pass, and that nothing happens without God planning it for the good of his people (Rom. 8:28; Eph. 1:22). Even failures of the past are part of God's plans for good. By learning from his past experiences of failure David grew in his knowledge of God and learned not to repeat them.

In 14:8-9 a very familiar pattern threatens to repeat itself in the life of Israel. The Philistines had a vested interest in keeping the kingdom of Israel divided and weak. Just as it had been in the best interests of the Philistines that David should undermine Saul, it was now in their interests that David should not rule over all Israel (14:8). They made a daring strike into Israelite territory, to within a few miles of the capital (14:9). This threatened to be a rerun of the Philistine advance that defeated Saul's army at Mount Gilboa. Would history repeat itself?

The problems that God's people face are often those that recur generation after generation. While specific temptations may take different forms in different ages and different cultures, the enemy we face is the Evil One who tempted Adam and Eve in the garden of Eden (see also Eccles. 1:9). Paul describes the temptations that lay hold of us as 'common to man' (1 Cor. 10:13). Many others have faced the trials we now face and those that confront us are to a degree predictable and recurring. We can never allow ourselves to imagine that once we have faced some particular trial it will not return to haunt us. Matthew Henry comments on these events with the following challenge: 'Let the attack which the Philistines made upon David forbid us to be secure in any settlement or advancement, and engage us to expect molestation.'

On this occasion David was able to learn from Saul's failure. Saul had responded to Philistine invasion by turning away from God and relying upon his own strength, while

David learned that there was no hope of salvation apart from God's strength and guidance. '**So David enquired of God: "Shall I go and attack the Philistines? Will you hand them over to me?"**' (14:10).

In the following verses we read of the victory that David won when he went up to engage the Philistines in battle in God's strength. The Philistines were defeated at a place called Baal Perazim, and their defeat was total (14:11). So complete was it that the Philistines abandoned their gods (14:12). Baal Perazim was not the original name of the place, but the one given to it after the battle because of the ferocity of God's assault upon the Philistines that day. The name means 'The Lord breaks out,' and is based on the Hebrew verb *parats*, which means 'to burst forth'. This verb was used to describe the breaking open of a barrel of water, the breaching of a wall during a siege, or the bursting of a dam, and in a military context it indicated a sudden, violent, devastating attack. One of the most spectacular successes of Allied bombers during the Second World War was the bombing of one of the dams in the Ruhr valley in Germany, causing torrents of water to flood the area below. David saw a similar outburst of the power of God upon the heads of his enemies at Baal Perazim.

Significantly the verb *parats* was also used in 13:11 when David had failed to bear the ark with due respect and the holy anger of God burst forth upon Uzzah. That place too was given a new name, Perez Uzzah, meaning 'the outbreak against Uzzah'. David had learned a lesson that day that he never forgot. He learned the hard way that the Lord God of heaven is a God of awesome holiness and mighty power. God will not permit his honour to be slighted with impunity, but will glorify his name in the destruction of those who despise him. When we learn lessons the hard way we are much more likely to remember them. After these two outbursts of God's power David was much more confident of God's strength when he went into battle against the enemies of the Lord. The God who had chastened him was also the God who was leading him into battle and on to victory.

Just as Moses assured the children of Israel as they crossed the Red Sea that 'The Egyptians you see today you will never see again. The Lord will fight for you' (Exod. 14:13-14), so God assured David that his strength would give him the victory. When David was in a right relationship with God the awesome power that had caused him to tremble now worked for him rather than against him. Never again would David have any reason to doubt God's power to overcome his enemies. Nor could David doubt the seriousness with which God looked upon any deviation from his law. As a result David destroyed the false 'gods' of the Philistines, whose 'help' had proved to be so pathetic compared with the power of the God of Israel (14:12).

It is said that we learn from our mistakes. Would that we did more often than we do! Too often Christians do not even acknowledge their mistakes or consider them so that they can learn lessons from them. This is like the boy who suffered from stomach cramps after eating stolen apples — because they were cooking apples. His father tried to use the opportunity to show the boy the difference between right and wrong and asked his son if he thought God was trying to teach him a lesson. 'Yes,' the boy replied, 'take them with sugar.' Aren't there times when we can be equally blind to the lessons that God would have us learn from our mistakes?

David was guided by God (14:13-17)

Not only did David learn from past failings, but he also moved forward from the scene of failure. Sometimes Christians can become bogged down in failures because they dwell on them.

The result is that they never grow out of them. The more we think about a thing, the more it influences us; and the more we think about sin and failure, the more these things imprison us in their grasp. This can be a very real obstacle preventing some people from growing into Christian maturity.

David moved on from failure by setting his mind on the things of God. He sought to know the will of God and how it applied to his life. He sought to establish patterns of godly behaviour in his daily routine, and the more he focused his thoughts upon these things, the more natural it became to him to do the right thing. We see in verse 13 how temptation returned in the form of another Philistine invasion. How would David respond to this renewed threat to his kingdom?

It would have been understandable if David had proceeded to repel the enemy as before. After all, the Lord had just recently demonstrated his power to help and the circumstances of this incursion were very similar. Yet David did not make any rash presumptions about what God might do, or whether God would assure him of victory. As David faced a new challenge he sought specific guidance for the situation in question. This time he found that God's guidance was slightly different from before. Instead of ordering a full frontal attack God said, **'Do not go straight up, but circle round them and attack them in front of the balsam trees. As soon as you hear the sound of marching in the tops of the balsam trees, move out to battle, because that will mean God has gone out in front of you to strike the Philistine army'** (14:14-15). David had to learn to seek God's guidance and to wait for God's signal before he could be assured that the victory would be his.

Here is an important lesson for the Christian to learn. Just as it is foolish to rely on an old map when travelling on a journey, so it is foolish to rely on 'old guidance' as we live the Christian life. Of course, the law of God never changes. There

are some courses of action that are *always* wrong, and some
precepts that are always to be insisted upon. For example, we
never need specific guidance not to steal, nor do we need it to
keep the Lord's Day holy. But as we seek to apply God's truth
to many other less clear-cut issues we need to be in constant
touch with our heavenly Father. Just as God gave the Israelites
food for each day in the wilderness, so that they would go back
each morning for nourishment, so God gives us direction for
each day as we renew our walk with him.

As we face new challenges and decisions each day we are
to take them all to God. As we begin a new day we may not
presume upon God's help unless we call upon him afresh. We
are to be like the servant whose eye was constantly on the
master:

> I lift up my eyes to you,
>   to you whose throne is in heaven.
> As the eyes of slaves look to the hand of their master,
>   as the eyes of a maid look to the hand of her mistress,
> so our eyes look to the Lord our God,
>   till he shows us his mercy
>
> (Ps. 123:1-2).

Then we discover that God's goodness is 'new every morning'
(Lam. 3:23).

11.
Bringing up the ark

Please read 1 Chronicles 15:1 - 16:3

If you have ever looked forward to a homecoming celebration you will appreciate the happiness described in this passage. Whenever friends or members of our family have been separated from us for a long time, there is excitement at the prospect of seeing them again. Although it is not accurate to describe this as the homecoming of the ark in the sense that (to the best of our knowledge, at least) it had not previously been kept in Jerusalem, it was now being brought to the place where it belonged — in other words, to its permanent home.

For the first time since the children of Israel had occupied the promised land the twelve tribes were united around one king and were secure in possession of their territory. The capture of Jerusalem from the Jebusites (see 11:4-9) was an event rich in significance and Zion became known as 'the City of David', the symbol of his monarchy. David wanted Jerusalem to be the centre, not only of the civic life of the nation, but also of the spiritual and religious life of God's people. Israel was 'one nation under God' and David was the Lord's anointed king over the Lord's people. He wanted the ark to be there in Jerusalem as a symbol of God's presence, truth and mercy in the midst of his people.

As we have already seen, David's laudable plan to bring the ark from its rather degrading place of storage in Kiriath Jearim

was initiated in 1 Chronicles 13 but it came to an abrupt and
tragic end after the death of Uzzah. God was angry with
David's carelessness in handling the ark. David had to learn to
approach the Lord's work with great reverence but, having
discovered that God is gracious as well as holy (13:14; 14:10-
11), he now sought to complete the journey and bring the ark
to Jerusalem. There were, however, some preparations that
had to be made before Jerusalem could be made the resting-
place for the ark.

A proper order had to be established (15:1-10)

At his first attempt David had sought to bring the ark to
Jerusalem on an ox-cart. To David this may have seemed a
very sensible and practical way of transporting the ark, but it
was not God's way. It was therefore the wrong way! Often our
sinful natures are attracted towards doing things 'our own
way'. We do not want to be governed by conventions we do not
understand; instead we want to stand on our own two feet and
make our own 'mature' decisions.

Attractive as the option of 'doing our own thing' often may
appear, it is, however, the very definition of sinful behaviour.
God has shown us how we are to live and serve him, but in our
sinful condition we prefer either to set his commands aside, or
to modify them to our liking. 'We all, like sheep, have gone
astray, each of us has turned to his own way' (Isa. 53:6). Our
way of serving God may take many different forms: it may be
false religion, or an attempt to earn God's favour by religious
works, or it may be a private quest for the divine that deliber-
ately ignores received truth in the Bible. Often men and
women take it ill when they are told that their own way can
never bring them into a right relationship with God, nor can it

be a proper way of serving God. 'He has showed you, O man, what is good' (Micah 6:8).

God had shown his people how they were to carry the ark of the covenant — on poles borne by the Levites on their shoulders (Exod. 25:13-15). There was a reminder of this in Numbers 7:9 when Moses did not give the Kohathites any carts or oxen to help with their work 'because they were to carry on their shoulders the holy things, for which they were responsible'. Why David failed to observe this command we do not know. Perhaps he was ignorant of this requirement, or had forgotten, or felt that it was too trivial an issue for God to be really concerned about. Perhaps he felt that he had liberty to update the instructions that God had given Moses. Whatever the reason, the fact is that David sinned in going beyond what God had laid down.

God did care about the way his instructions were regarded and does not give us liberty to add or discard what we might see fit in our worship and service for him. This is a principle that seems so obvious that it should hardly have to be argued, yet there is a continual urge in the human heart to push at the boundaries of God's law and ask, 'Did God really say that?' The fallen human mind is full of ideas about how we might 'enrich' the worship of God, but they are not God's ideas. David learned this principle and started applying it in the religious life of his people.

He first laid down a rule: **'No one but the Levites may carry the ark of God, because the Lord chose them to carry the ark of the Lord and to minister before him for ever'** (15:2). Then in verse 4 we read how David assembled the Levites to update them on the new policy and in verses 5-10 a roster of the Levites who were eligible for this work is listed. The thoroughness of this record shows how seriously the issue was taken. This may sound like a detail of organization, but it

is more than that. It shows a right attitude to the holy things of
God. God's people ought to be moved by a love for God and
his Word to see that their worship and church life are brought
into close conformity to God's revealed will. In the history of
the church structural reorganization has often accompanied
spiritual renewal. At the time of the Protestant Reformation in
the sixteenth century many ceremonies and corruptions were
eliminated because they were not commanded, or sanctioned,
in the Word of God. As David discovered, these additions are
a hindrance to blessing, and must be discarded before God's
blessing can be more fully enjoyed.

Personal consecration (15:11-15)

David was painfully aware that as king he had not given proper
leadership to his people. Laxity had been allowed to creep into
the religious life of the Israelites. His desire was that some of
the most obvious failures might be remedied and a new system
established to ensure that past sins would not be repeated.
There was, however, a concern even more pressing than the
organizational one, for the people's hearts must be reformed
if they were to enjoy God's blessing. So in verses 11-15 David
spoke to the Levites and urged a thorough examination of their
hearts.

The low ebb of spiritual life that David inherited affected
every section of the people of God. Even the Levites, who were
to be the conscience of the nation, had failed to exercise a
leavening influence within it. It was their responsibility to
make sure that the people were instructed in God's precepts so
that an incident like that at Perez Uzzah did not happen. David
reminded them that they had been found wanting: **'It was
because you, the Levites, did not bring it up the first time
that the Lord our God broke out in anger against us'**

(15:13). Moreover David gathered the heads of the priestly and Levitical families and urged them to take responsibility for their families: **'You are the heads of the Levitical families; you and your fellow Levites are to consecrate yourselves and bring up the ark of the Lord, the God of Israel, to the place I have prepared for it'** (15:11-12).

Fathers and heads of families have a responsibility, not just for their own spiritual growth, but to seek the growth in grace of those under their care. No father can regenerate or sanctify his children, nor can he believe and obey the gospel in their place, but he has a great influence upon their spiritual development, for good or for ill. A parent's teaching and example (and this applies to mothers as well as fathers) are probably the strongest influences on children as they grow up (see Prov. 22:6; 2 Tim. 3:14-15). Paul urged fathers: 'Do not exasperate your children; instead, bring them up in the training and instruction of the Lord' (Eph. 6:4). Children so trained will know the commands God gives and what it means to obey them, but they will also know what it is to love the Lord and will desire to consecrate their lives to him.

Consecration is the duty of all God's people, and is the prerequisite of blessed fellowship with him. When the Lord God came down on Mount Sinai, Moses commanded the people to consecrate themselves before the Lord would speak to them (Exod. 19:10). Often in the Old Testament this meant washing the body and clothes, avoiding contact with dead bodies, abstaining from intimate relations, or anything else that caused ceremonial defilement. Anyone ceremonially defiled was barred from entering the temple to offer a sacrifice. For these Levites consecration meant putting away anything that smacked of past disobedience, laziness or carelessness about their sacred duties. Consecration was a recommitment in their hearts to the work to which the Lord had set them apart (15:14-15).

How we live as God's people is a matter of great importance
to God and has a profound impact on the quality of our
relationship with him. Jonathan Edwards wrote of the ambition which dominated his Christian life, 'It was my continual strife day and night, and constant enquiry, how I should
be more holy, and live more holily, and more becoming a
child of God and a disciple of Christ. I now sought an increase
of grace and holiness, and a holy life, with much more
earnestness than I ever sought before I had it.' A person who
professes to be a Christian but shows little of this concern for
holiness of heart and life cannot expect much enjoyment of
God in his salvation.

Imagine the person who receives an invitation to a Royal
Garden Party at Buckingham Palace, but is so excited that in
the rush to attend he forgets to wear the proper dress. His
excitement would continue until he arrived at the palace gate
and noticed how out of place he looked beside the other guests
arriving in morning dress. He would notice how others stared
at him, and how incongruous he appeared. That would not be
a pleasant way to spend an afternoon! So it is with those who
approach the Lord of heaven (1 Tim. 6:16) with no concern for
their personal holiness. Progress in holiness is our preparation
to enter the holy presence of God, and is inseparable from the
enjoyment of salvation: 'Make every effort to live in peace
with all men and to be holy; without holiness no one will see
the Lord' (Heb. 12:14; see also Matt. 22:11-13).

Of course, it is equally impossible for any who are truly
born again and truly converted to Christ, cleansed from their
sins and adopted into the family of God not to make progress
in sanctification from the time of their conversion until the
moment they enter God's presence, when every trace of sin
will finally be removed from their lives (see 1 Cor. 6:11; Phil.
1:6; Rom. 8:29-30).

A rejoicing people (15:16-24)

These verses describe the preparations that were made to receive the ark when it would arrive in Jerusalem. Extensive preparations are made when an important person, or sometimes even his representative, visits a town. When in November 1995 the President of the United States of America visited Belfast to encourage the 'peace process' many months of hard work had taken place in preparation for the visit of one very important man and his entourage of 700 people. These preparations serve to highlight the importance of such an occasion.

The arrival of the ark in Jerusalem was an event of great significance to David and his people, because it marked Jerusalem as God's 'resting-place' (Ps. 132:7-8). As a result the priests and people showed their joyful appreciation of God's goodness to them (Ps. 132:9). There was a spontaneous outpouring of rejoicing as the ark was brought up, but these verses also show that this spontaneous movement was directed by the Word of God so that it was a truly edifying occasion. David asked the Levites to appoint some of their number to sing songs of praise (15:16). Among the singers were the famous trio of Heman, Asaph and Ethan who (as we saw in our study of chapter 6) wrote some of the songs in the book of Psalms.

Others were appointed to blow trumpets as the ark was carried (15:24). As when the ark was carried around Jericho (Josh. 6:16) and at the beginning of certain festivals (Lev. 23:24; 25:9), the blowing of trumpets was a signal calling the attention of the people to God's mighty acts of deliverance. In this case the trumpets heralded God's goodness in making Jerusalem his earthly dwelling-place. A 'holy place' was being established amongst the nations of the earth, for God had chosen one nation to be his special people.

In the midst of his chosen people God had commanded that a special meeting-place be built where God and his people could meet. Initially this was the tabernacle, but when Jerusalem was secured as the nation's capital a temple was to be built there. This was to be the 'holy place'. Because the holy place was to be kept holy doorkeepers would be needed to keep defilement out of God's presence (15:23-24). We shall consider the importance of their role later, but as we study these verses we take note of the appointment of men to this role early in David's reign. The Obed-Edom mentioned in verse 24 is probably not the same man as Obed-Edom the Gittite, who looked after the ark for three months after the death of Uzzah (13:14), because he was from Levite stock.

We should notice the importance of the singing of praise in the worship of God. Although an array of musical instruments was used to accompany the singing of praise (15:16,19-21), the primary commission of the Levites was **'to sing joyful songs'** (15:16). Matthew Henry comments on this balance of priorities: 'The New Testament keeps up the singing of Psalms, but has not appointed church music.' The importance of singing such songs of praise is that as well as ascribing due honour to God they instruct the minds and edify the souls of those present. Praise is not 'sanctified entertainment', nor is it simply a minor preliminary to more important elements of public worship. It is as important as prayer, reading and preaching of the Word. As we sing praise we are instructed ourselves and we instruct others in the greatness of our God and Saviour. With this end in view, Paul encouraged the church to 'speak to one another with psalms, hymns and spiritual songs' (Eph. 5:19).

The importance of praise means that it should be offered to the very best of our ability. We read that **'Kenaniah the head Levite was in charge of the singing'** and that this **'was his responsibility because he was skilful at it'** (15:22). Two technical terms are used in describing the arrangements in verses 20-21: *alamoth*, which refers to 'girls' voices', probably means treble or soprano, and *sheminith*, which refers to an octave or interval of eight notes, probably means tenor or bass. The use of these technical terms indicates a certain musical sophistication. The Levites had dedicated their skills to improving the quality of their praise as much as they could.

This is only as it should be because God's people have a duty to dedicate their gifts to the glory of God and should train themselves so that their praise is as honouring to God as it can be. J. P. Struthers, whose Reformed Presbyterian Congregation in Greenock, Scotland, sang the Psalms without instrumental accompaniment, used to urge his people to make their singing so rich and sweet that passers-by would be compelled to stop and say, 'Listen to the angels singing!'

The way of sacrifice (15:25 - 16:4)

There was one final preparation that David needed to make before he could bring the ark into Jerusalem. Thus far we have seen how David reformed the religious life of his nation, encouraged personal holiness and led the people in an expression of devotion to God. These measures presume that an angry God can be made favourable to sinful people. The consistent message of Scripture is that this cannot take place without the shedding of sacrificial blood: 'Without the shedding of blood there is no forgiveness' (Heb. 9:22), and without forgiveness nothing we offer to God can be accepted, however painstakingly we offer it. The weight of our sinfulness hangs like a millstone around our necks as sinners, and offends God every minute we live.

In these verses David and his people offer sacrifices before they bring the symbol of God's holiness into their midst

(15:26; 16:1-2). Either the sinner must bear the anger of God, or a suitable substitute must stand in his place. In the years before the substitutionary work of 'Christ our Passover' was properly understood the blood of sacrificial animals was shed to point to the provision that God in his grace would make for sinners by the sacrifice of his Son. The 'burnt offering' spoke of the removal of sin and guilt, while the 'fellowship offering' spoke of the privileges which God's people came to enjoy (16:1).

David's offerings emphasized the importance of the priestly ministry. In verse 27 he even wore a linen ephod, a priestly garment, as he walked with the Levites. This is not to imply that David had usurped the priestly prerogative of offering sacrifices, as Saul had done to his cost in 1 Samuel 13:9. David's action symbolized the importance of the priestly ministry and his identification with the Levites, entrenching their importance in the life of the nation.

With what joy David and his people must have rejoiced as they thought about the significance of what was happening before their eyes! They were no longer under the wrath of God, but able by his grace to enjoy fellowship with him. How this 'amazing grace' made David's heart leap within him — and he let the world see it! 'Now to the King eternal, immortal, invisible, the only God, be honour and glory for ever and ever. Amen' (1 Tim. 1:17). Unfortunately not everyone in Israel that day saw things as David did!

Postscript (15:29)

What a contrast between the heart of David, overflowing with devotion to God so that he danced and celebrated, and the heart of Michal his wife! She **'despised him in her heart'** when she saw his behaviour. We can see two influences at work in Michal's heart.

1. The influence of Saul on his daughter

Michal was Saul's daughter and obviously shared his attitude to spiritual matters. Saul had shown contempt for the ark of the Lord (13:3) and passed his contempt on to his daughter. The harsh, cynical, bitter and even unguarded words that parents say can have quite unexpected consequences in the years to come in the lives of their children.

2. The hostility that devotion to God provokes from godless people

The more David expressed his devotion to God, the more he goaded Michal in her rebellion against God. David's warmth exposed her coldness, and she responded as godless people often do — by despising those who goad their consciences. This is illustrative of the hostility that real Christianity evokes from those whose religion is false and external. We should be prepared for such a reaction, for such temporary contempt from the world is a small price to pay compared with the privileges of fellowship with God. David could have echoed the thoughts of Paul, who was rejected by his own people because of his devotion to the God of Israel: 'I consider that our present sufferings are not worth comparing with the glory that will be revealed in us' (Rom. 8:18).

12.
A psalm of praise

Please read 1 Chronicles 16:4-43

The experience of many Christians is marked by peaks of blessing and troughs of weakness. There will be occasional 'mountaintop experiences' and descents into the valley of despair, but our lives are spent mainly on the plateau of daily, and apparently uneventful, Christian living. It is important to draw strength from the times of great blessing that will sustain us through the discouraging and the routine times.

The day when King David led his people in bringing up the ark of the Lord to Jerusalem was a time of great blessing. God's presence, symbolized by the ark, was enjoyed in great measure that day. The Chronicler records that 'David and the elders of Israel and the commanders of units of a thousand went to bring up the ark of the covenant of the Lord from the house of Obed-Edom, with rejoicing' (15:25).

David did not want the blessings of that day to slip into history leaving no mark on the spiritual life, or even the memory, of his people. He wanted them to remember what they had experienced of God's goodness and as a result to grow in their devotion to the Lord. It would not be possible for them to live for ever on the spiritual mountaintop, but David sought to establish patterns of true worship so that his people would continue to seek the Lord and enjoy his blessing. This they would do as they remembered the Lord their God and gave thanks for his past goodness to them. This passage describes the measures David took to encourage this.

David taught the people to be a praying people (16:4-6)

When a Westerner visits an Islamic country one of the features of daily life that he finds most striking is the regular cry of the muezzin calling his co-religionists to prayer five times a day. The equivalent in England might be the peal of church bells which call worshippers to the house of God. In Old Testament times it was the sounding of trumpets that called the people to prayer. The sound of trumpets had been associated in Israel's history with God's mighty acts of redemption. The same sound that heralded God's miraculous goodness called those who had been blessed to worship their Lord. David appointed Levites to give form and organization to the worship of his people, and one of their duties was **'to blow the trumpets regularly before the ark of the covenant of God'** (16:5-6).

More details of this ministry are given in verse 4, where we are told that David **'appointed some of the Levites to minister before the ark of the Lord'**. As the offering of animal sacrifices was the special work of the family of Aaron, the particular responsibility of these Levites was to lead the prayers of the people, and specifically **'to make petition, to give thanks, and to praise the Lord, the God of Israel'**. In these three phrases we have an excellent summary of the essentials of true prayer.

1. Petitions

Prayer will include petitions or requests, but not for frivolous or selfish things. The Hebrew word used here is a form of the verb *zachar*, to remember, for the petitioner is causing God to remember the promises that he has made to his people. This is how Nehemiah prayed while his people were in exile: 'O Lord, God of heaven, the great and awesome God, who keeps his covenant of love with those who love him... Remember the instruction you gave your servant Moses, saying, "If you are unfaithful, I will scatter you among the nations, but if you return to me and obey my commands, then even if your exiled people are at the farthest horizon, I will gather them from there and bring them to the place I have chosen as a dwelling for my Name"' (Neh. 1:5,8-9). We know that we are praying for 'things according to his will' when we plead his promises before him in prayer.

2. Thanksgiving

There will also be an element of thanksgiving. The word that is used here is a joyful one, meaning 'to sing, to celebrate, to declare in praise'. At the root of true worship is not a vague sense of well-being, but a remembrance of the many good things that God has done for us (see Ps. 40:5; 71:15-18; 98:1-3).

3. Praise

True prayer will also include praise. From the Hebrew word used here we derive the expression 'Hallelujah' or 'Praise the Lord'. Because the Lord is great and powerful we worship God for who he is, as well as what he has done for us. This was the perspective of Job when he said, 'Though he slay me, yet will I hope in him' (Job 13:15). Without this perspective prayer revolves around us, our joys and our pains, and ceases to be true worship which centres on God, his perfections and his goodness. The balance of these verses is commended to us by the apostle Paul when he writes, 'In everything, by prayer and petition, with thanksgiving, present your requests to God' (Phil. 4:6).

David showed his people how to praise God (16:7-36)

One of the most abiding legacies from the life of King David has proved to be the songs of praise that are preserved in the book of Psalms. In his own day David was recognized for his musical gifts (1 Sam. 16:23) and these gifts were dedicated to the Lord's service. He was described as 'the man anointed by the God of Jacob, Israel's singer of songs' or, as translated in the Authorized Version, 'the sweet psalmist of Israel' (2 Sam. 23:1). Yet he was no ordinary singer and songwriter. His work was done under the supervision of the Holy Spirit so that his psalms were recognized as nothing less than the Word of God: 'The Spirit of the Lord spoke through me; his word was on my tongue' (2 Sam. 23:2; cf. 2 Peter 1:21). For this reason the psalms have provided a treasury of spiritual blessing for generations of God's people ever since.

In the passage before us we have the enlightened reflections of a godly heart following a day of great blessing. Lest the people forget the lessons that had been learned that day, David committed them to Asaph and his fellow Levites to be recorded in writing (literally, 'by the hand of Asaph and his brothers') and remembered in Israel's praise. Three themes in this passage call for special mention.

1. The mighty acts of God in the past (16:8-13; cf. Ps. 105:1-6)

Twice in these verses the expression **'wonderful acts'** or **'wonders'** is used (16:9,12) and this sets the tone for the passage. The Hebrew word used means 'actions that cause wonder', or simply 'miracles'. Because of these the Lord, who is 'wonderful' (Isa. 9:6), is greatly to be praised.

Certainly there were many miraculous deeds that God's people could remember from their national experience: the burning bush, the Exodus, their preservation in the wilderness, their entry into the promised land. The ark had been associated with some of these events — for instance, the crossing of the river Jordan and the collapse of the walls of Jericho. Now they were rejoicing in the miracle of forgiveness and reconciliation between God and his sinful people represented by the ark's arrival in Jerusalem. The ark that had amazed the people with its destructive potential now caused them to rejoice that the God of all power was their God and their Redeemer.

2. *The covenant faithfulness of God* (16:14-22; cf. Ps. 105:7-15)

The ark was the most visible and the most sacred symbol of God's covenant with his people, and in this psalm David expands upon the theme of God's covenant, which is an everlasting covenant, revealed to Abraham, Isaac and Jacob (16:16-17) and confirmed to their descendants. God did not enter into covenant with his people because they were impressive or worthy or numerous (16:19; cf. Deut. 7:7-8); nor was it because he needed them, but because he loved them!

The ark contained the *terms* of God's covenant — the law which they were to keep faithfully as their response to his goodness. God's promises are linked to a command (16:15), and his commandments were proclaimed from Mount Sinai after their deliverance from Egypt. There were many warnings about disobedience, or covenant-breaking: 'Be sure to keep the commands of the Lord your God and the stipulations and the decrees he has given you. Do what is right and good in the Lord's sight, so that it may go well with you and you may go in and take over the good land that the Lord promised on oath to your forefathers' (Deut. 6:17-18). 'But if you will not listen to me and carry out all these commands, and if you reject my decrees and abhor my laws and fail to carry out all my commands and so violate my covenant, then I will do this to you: I will bring upon you sudden terror, wasting diseases and fever that will destroy your sight and drain away your life' (Lev. 26:14-16).

There is another lesson about God's covenant that David has discovered: the blessings of fellowship with God are not earned by our faithfulness but rather are enjoyed in spite of our failings. God's eternal love is the basis on which every blessing rests. David had sinned and had brought well-deserved chastisement upon himself, but the covenant love of God cleansed away his guilt and restored the joy of his salvation. This is because God **'remembers his covenant for ever'** (16:15). Although his people wander from him they will never be cast off utterly. He allows **'no man to oppress them'** and commands, **'Do not touch my anointed ones; do my prophets no harm'** (16:21-22). God's covenant love is more powerful to save than our sin is powerful to destroy.

3. The universal dominion of God (16: 23-36; cf. Ps. 96:1-13; 106:1,47-48).

In these verses David looks beyond the boundaries of his own nation and calls upon all people everywhere to praise God: **'Sing to the Lord, all the earth; proclaim his salvation day after day'** (16:23).

It was commonly believed in the ancient world that there were many gods, constantly struggling for pre-eminence.

Even some Israelites had the idea that, while their own God was greater than the rest, these lesser gods were real and each had their territory and their people to serve them. David would not allow the Israelites to think like that, even for a moment. The Lord Jehovah is the God of the heavens and the earth. He cannot even for a moment be likened to those false gods. He is unique, the only God, and David proclaimed that truth when he said, **'Declare ... his marvellous deeds among all peoples'** (16:24). It is a disgrace to the true God to imagine that any nation can be abandoned to the sway of false gods: **'He is to be feared above all gods.'** Therefore, urged David, **'Ascribe to the Lord, O families of nations ... glory and strength'** (16:25,28). The Lord of Israel is a God of universal dominion, claiming universal adoration.

Imagine how that truth would have spoken to the Chronicler's generation, when the people of Israel were scattered as exiles throughout the ancient world. Israel was no longer a great nation, but a small province of the Persian empire. There was no ark, and a much smaller temple than in the nation's heyday, but their God was still the Lord of all the earth. God had warned his people that they would be scattered from their homeland if they were unfaithful to him (2 Chron. 7:19-20; Jer. 9:16). But along with that warning there was always the promise that their time of punishment would be followed by a period of restoration (2 Chron. 7:14; Isa. 11:12).

Just as a shepherd cannot bear to see the scattered and vulnerable sheep from his flock left in the wilderness but goes out to rescue them, so God showed his love for Israel by gathering her scattered children from their exile. 'He tends his flock like a shepherd: he gathers the lambs in his arms' (Isa. 40:11; 49:5; 56:8; Jer. 23:3). God's unchanging mercy had a very special relevance to those Israelites living after the exile who had seen their nation scattered throughout their known

world (see also Mal. 3:6). They were urged to cry out to God
for relief:

> **Cry out, 'Save us, O God our Saviour;**
> **gather us and deliver us from the nations,**
> **that we may give thanks to your holy name,**
> **that we may glory in your praise'**
>
> (16:35).

The gathering of the exiles from out of many nations was
indeed a wonderful cause of national rejoicing!

Today God gathers his elect from amongst the people of
every nation (Matt. 8:11; 1 Peter 1:1) by the preaching of the
gospel of Christ, and there is heavenly rejoicing when even
one sinner is gathered into the number of those who believe
(Luke 15:2). God's people ought not to tremble as they face the
hostility of a godless world. Rather, as David said,

> **Tremble before him, all the earth!**
> **The world is firmly established; it cannot be**
> **moved.**
> **Let the heavens rejoice, let the earth be glad;**
> **let them say among the nations, 'The Lord**
> **reigns!'**
>
> (16:30-31).

To all these truths the people respond with a heartfelt
'Amen'. Our hearts should be stirred to prayer as we remember that our prayers ascend to a Hearer whose miraculous
power can never be exhausted. We need not fear his reproach
because his covenant goodness cannot be exhausted. Neither
is there is any place to which we can go, or be taken, where we
are not within the boundaries of his sovereign power. To these

certainties we say 'Amen' as we worship the true and eternal
God of whom David speaks in this psalm.

David appointed leaders responsible for leading the people's worship (16:37-43)

All good things must come to an end, and it must have been
with a hint of sadness that David and the Israelites went home
that evening exhausted but exhilarated: **'Then all the people
left, each for his own home, and David returned home to
bless his family'** (16:43). They went to share the blessings of
that day with their children, that they too might know of the
mercies of the Lord. Yet the worship of God would not cease
as the crowd of worshippers dispersed. David saw to it that a
pattern of worship was established to continue thereafter. He
appointed **'Asaph and his associates ... to minister there** [in
Jerusalem] **regularly, according to each day's requirements'** (16:37), and verse 7 seems to indicate that Asaph's
special ministry can be dated to this particular day.

Neither did David forget the sacrifices that God had appointed to be offered at the tabernacle, now located at Gibeon.
One of the constant features of spiritual declension in Israel
was that these sacrifices were ignored, or offered infrequently.
David appointed Zadok the priest **'to present burnt offerings
to the Lord on the altar of burnt offering regularly,
morning and evening, in accordance with everything written in the Law of the Lord'** (16:40). As well as being *regular*
the worship of God was *regulated* by his express instructions
so that it might be pleasing to him.

In spite of David's reforms the worship of Israel was still
irregular in one important way. The sacrifices at the tabernacle
were separated from the ark of God's presence. The means of

entry into God's presence (the blood shed at the tabernacle) was separated from the symbol of God's presence (the ark) because there was as yet no central place of worship at which all Israel might gather. The Lord had promised such a place to Moses in Deuteronomy 12:11-14. The people were not to devise a place for themselves but were to wait until God would lead them to it. In the absence of clear guidance a series of 'high places' sprang up throughout Israel, in some instances at the places where the pagan Canaanites had worshipped. Here the people offered sacrifices. Shiloh was one such place and it was there that Eli the high priest ministered (1 Sam. 1:3). Another was Ramah, where Samuel judged Israel and built an altar to the Lord (1 Sam. 7:17).

Gibeon was another high place which came to the fore after the family of Eli had been destroyed and the tabernacle relocated after the disaster of 1 Samuel 4. It came to be known as 'the great high place', and it was to Gibeon that Solomon called the people at the beginning of his reign to worship the Lord (2 Chron. 1:3). Here it was that the tabernacle stood and the people came to offer sacrifices. Yet the ark was kept in another tent in Jerusalem (see 16:1).

David's desire was that a sanctuary might be built at which all Israel would gather to offer sacrifices and within which the ark of the covenant might be kept. The story of the construction of such a temple is taken up in the following chapter and comes to dominate the Chronicler's history. In this temple the means whereby sinners can come into God's presence, represented by the sacrificial offerings, and the ark, which symbolized God's presence, are brought into close physical proximity, indicating the accessibility of God's covenant blessings.

Ultimately, the end of our salvation and the means whereby it is achieved are brought into an even closer union in the person of Jesus Christ, the mediator of the new covenant whose shed blood opened a 'new and living way' to God. The moment of his death was marked by the tearing open of the temple veil which until then had sealed off the most holy place (containing the ark of the covenant) from the priests and the people of Israel. Now, when we make our approach to God through the way of Christ's cross, all the blessings of forgiveness and acceptance are made immediately available to even the chief of sinners.

13.
God's covenant with David

Please read 1 Chronicles 17:1-27

Some people have a temper that is rash and bold; they are
choleric rather than phlegmatic, impulsive rather than calcu-
lating. In this type of personality there are many strengths, for
these are the people who get things done. But there is also a
great drawback, for the impulsive person can rush unwittingly
into foolish mistakes. Saul of Tarsus, who showed his zeal by
persecuting the church, and Simon Peter, who often spoke
before he thought, were impulsive men who did harm to the
church as well as much good.

King David was a man who, as we have seen, was fired by
a great desire to serve the Lord. Having gathered his people,
he led them in a joyful procession as the ark of the Lord was
transported from Kiriath Jearim to Jerusalem, the capital of his
newly united kingdom. As his kingdom grew in power and
dignity David wanted to build a temple to show that the Lord
God was at the centre of it, building it for his glory. This
ambition was thwarted by the Lord himself, and this must have
been a surprise to David. How would this impulsive man react
to having his ambitions so unexpectedly checked by God?

As we study this chapter we see that, while God closed one
door to David, he opened another. Although David would not
be remembered as the man who built the temple, he would be
known as the father of the Messianic line. God renewed his

covenant with his people by promising David a son who would make his kingdom an everlasting kingdom. Some have called this chapter the very heart of the Chronicler's history, even one of the most important chapters in the Old Testament. Certainly David's desire to build a temple was enlarged into a prayer for Messianic blessing.

David's desire (17:1-2)

It is impossible to fault David for the ambition he shared with Nathan: **'Here I am, living in a palace of cedar, while the ark of the covenant of the Lord is under a tent'** (17:1). The contrast seemed to David to be incongruous, to say the least, if not actually insulting to the Lord of heaven. After all, it was God who had given David every blessing that he enjoyed — including his palace of cedar. David's heart prompted him to build a temple for the ark of the Lord.

When Nathan heard David's plan he was impressed and, speaking as a prophet, sought to assure the king of God's blessing: **'Whatever you have in mind, do it, for God is with you'** (17:2). These words must have warmed David's heart because Nathan was certainly no 'yes man' who said what he was expected to say. He was a man of great wisdom and courage, for it was he who rebuked David for murdering Uriah and committing adultery with Bathsheba. It was Nathan who said, 'You are the man!' (2 Sam. 12:7) and who would later risk his life to ensure that Solomon succeeded to the throne rather than Adonijah (1 Kings 1:38). So we can be sure that Nathan was not simply humouring David when he spoke these words of encouragement.

David's desire to build a house for the ark of the Lord was a good and genuine one and Nathan recognized the sincerity and the worthiness of his plans. It was God's intention that such a temple should be built eventually, and David was a man 'after God's own heart', but it was not David who would build the temple. Again we see how a good man can be genuinely mistaken, and how important it is to seek the Lord's guidance *before* we embark on a project. The *attitude* in which we seek God's guidance is equally important, for it is pointless asking God for guidance if we are not willing to be corrected by him.

God's reply (17:3-15)

Before David could begin to implement his plans, **'The word of God came to Nathan'** (17:3) with instructions that he was not to build the temple. If David was disappointed by this news, he must have been heartened by the explanation that accompanied it. God explained to Nathan why his plans were greater even than David's.

1. God's honour does not depend on magnificent buildings (17:4-6)

There was not the urgency that David had imagined for a temple to be built for the Lord. After all, the people of Israel had seen the mighty works of God and marvelled at his greatness for hundreds of years without the aid of a temple. Looking back to the Exodus, God said, **'I have not dwelt in a house from the day I brought Israel up out of Egypt to this day'** (17:5). The same was true all through the wilderness years (17:6). God is a spirit who cannot be contained in the whole created universe, let alone an earthly temple.

There was the constant danger in Israel that people would think of a temple, or some other structure, as an automatic means of blessing. This created a false sense of confidence (see Jer. 7:4) and it dishonoured God, because the God of heaven cannot be limited to any earthly place as his dwelling. There was no essential requirement for the people of God to have a special building as a means of blessing, for the place God delights to be is where faithful people call upon his name in truth and sincerity (Ps. 149:2).

2. God takes the initiative in unfolding his plan of salvation (17:7-10)

As we read these verses we should notice how God empha- sized that it was his initiative which had shaped David's life: **'I took you from the pasture... I have been with you wherever you have gone, and I have cut off all your enemies from before you... And I will provide a place for my people Israel...'** (17:7-9). This is the pattern of God's dealings with his people.

These verses illustrate the sad reality that we are prone to forget that God's goodness to us is undeserved and comes at his merciful initiative. God does not choose people to serve him because they are more gifted or virtuous than others. He chooses sinners who are totally unworthy of his salvation (Rom. 5:6-8; 1 John 4:10), even hostile to his plans (1 Cor. 2:14), and he takes into his service many who are despised by the world (1 Cor. 1:26-29). This had been true of Saul (although he forgot it). God, speaking through the prophet Samuel, reminded him of it: 'Although you were once small in your own eyes, did you not become the head of the tribes of Israel? The Lord anointed you king over Israel' (1 Sam. 15:17).

David was not to be allowed to forget that he had become what he was because of God's gracious initiative in his life. God had taken him from looking after a few sheep in the Judean wilderness and placed him on the throne of Israel (17:7). Everything that David had accomplished was because

God had gone before him preparing the way (17:8). His future had been mapped out by God (17:9). David needed to learn that God had not finished taking the lead in his life. There were many more good things that God had in store for David and his people which would be revealed in God's good time. There were more enemies who would be subdued under the Lord's people and, yes, a temple would be built (17:9-10). But Nathan's message was: **'I declare to you that the Lord will build a house for you.'** When that time came God would again take the initiative.

3. God would give David a son who would build an everlasting kingdom (17:11-15)

These verses are the climax of this chapter and the centrepiece of God's covenant with David. In the covenant God made with David there are four elements:

A son from David's offspring would succeed him (17:11).
That son would build God's house (17:12).
That son would enjoy a special relationship with God (17:13).
His kingdom would be an everlasting kingdom (17:14).

Only later in the Chronicles account is this promise linked to Solomon (22:9-10; 28:5-6). Initially the Chronicler allows us to consider the promise of a son in its glorious simplicity so that we might consider some aspects of God's dealings that we might otherwise overlook.

We notice that even a gifted and godly man like David was not able to do everything he might want to do. Although David was wealthy, willing and materially well equipped to build a house for the Lord in Jerusalem, God said that he was not the man to do that job. There are avenues of service that remain closed to us, because that is how God has planned it. A famous instance of that happening was the blindness of John Milton, the poet. Milton's active involvement in English political life was brought to an end when God took away his sight. That affliction did not end Milton's usefulness, but it prompted him to devote his energies to writing poetry. As a result he wrote some of the finest poetry in the English language, reflecting on the themes of sin and redemption. God does not always show us why he closes some doors to us, but it is a mark of grace to accept the limitations he places on us.

We must also notice the prominence given to family relationships in these verses. God promised David that he would give him **'offspring'** and that one of these sons would sit on his throne. This privileged son will **'build a house'** and **'his house'** will be **'established for ever'** (17:12,23). The word 'house' in this passage refers not just to a building, but to a family. Here is a very typical Hebrew play on words, for the most lasting legacy that this son would leave would not be a building of stone and timber, but a family of living people that would pass the truths of God's grace from one generation to the next. That is why faithfulness in training the rising generation in the home is so strongly emphasized, and failings in this regard have such serious consequences.

Although he is not mentioned by name in these verses, they look forward to the reign of Solomon, who would succeed David as King of Israel. Solomon was David's chosen successor, and it was he who would both build a house of worship for the Lord and preserve David's family line. He enjoyed a special relationship with God, receiving a unique gift of wisdom and being honoured with the title 'Jedidiah', or 'the one loved by the Lord' (2 Sam. 12:25; Neh. 13:26). What makes us look beyond Solomon as we read these verses is the promise of an everlasting kingdom: **'I will set him over my house and my kingdom for ever; his throne will be established for ever'** (17:14). We know that Solomon's kingdom was divided shortly after his death and by the time that the Chronicler was writing Judea occupied only a fraction of the territory of Solomon's empire.

The promise of a son to David was the unfolding of an even older promise. There had been the hope of a coming Saviour ever since the Fall and God's promise that the seed of the woman would crush the head of the serpent (Gen. 3:15). Now, as well as looking for 'the seed of the woman', God's people would await a king who was 'the son of David'. These promises were fulfilled in the person of the Lord Jesus Christ who was born both of a virgin and of 'the house and line of David' (Luke 2:4; Rom. 1:3). The Lord Jesus astounded the Jews by his claim that he would build a new temple in three days, referring to his body (John 2:20-21) and his church (Eph. 2:21; 1 Peter 2:5). His dominion over all things is the kingdom that can never end. He will be victorious over all his enemies (Phil. 2:9-11; Rev. 11:15).

We might ask how much David understood of this promise. The depth of insight shown in his Messianic psalms shows that David certainly rejoiced to look forward to the day of Christ. The covenant promise recorded in 1 Chronicles 17 and 2 Samuel 7 provided the basis for his hope. David spoke of a son who was more than a son for he was called 'Lord' (Ps. 110:1; Luke 20:41-44). He also knew of a son who would enjoy a relationship with his heavenly Father, even more glorious than that between a sinner and his Saviour. When the writer to the Hebrews quoted Psalm 2:7 he asked, 'To which of the angels did God ever say, "You are my Son; today I have become your Father?"' (Heb. 1:5). Similarly in Psalm 45 he speaks of an everlasting kingdom: 'Your throne, O God, will last for ever and ever, and righteousness will be the sceptre of

your kingdom' (Heb. 1:8-9; cf. Ps. 45:6-7). Psalm 132 was
David's own summary of this covenant promise and it com-
bines the blessings of salvation with the royal dignity of the
Messiah:

> I will clothe her priests with salvation,
>   and her saints shall ever sing for joy.
> Here I will make a horn grow for David
>   and set up a lamp for my anointed one.
> I will clothe his enemies with shame,
>   but the crown on his head shall be resplendent
>   (Ps. 132:16-18).

David's prayer (17:16-27)

David's prayer in these verses is a model of submissiveness to
God's revealed will. Point by point, David took Nathan's
message and made it a reason for praise and thanksgiving.
There was no hint of David's being disappointed by what God
had told him. His enthusiasm was in no way diminished, but
redirected more properly to reflect God's will. I can think of
a man who showed great generosity to students for the ministry by giving them books. His reason was that the Lord had not
called him to be a preacher, but if he could help those who were
so called that was sufficient for him. David showed that
generous spirit as he prayed according to these verses.

1. He acknowledged his personal unworthiness (17:16-19)

**'Who am I, O Lord God, and what is my family, that you
have brought me this far? ... You have looked on me as
though I were the most exalted of men'** (17:16-17). These
words give us an interesting insight into the grace of God. By

nature we are sinners who have forfeited any claim on God's mercy. If God were to treat us as we deserved we would instantly be stripped of every blessing and swept into eternal torment (Ps. 130:3). But God, in mercy, does not treat us as we deserve; instead he holds out forgiveness in the gospel and regards those who believe on the Lord Jesus Christ as his children (1 John 3:1). This is a work of grace that should constantly cause us to marvel before God, just as David marvelled in these verses. Not only had God exalted David from his low position, he would exalt David yet further, announcing that his son would be the Messianic king.

2. He acknowledged God's priorities (17:20-24)

There was (and is) no God like the God of Israel, for he is the only true God (17:20). His priorities are very different from those attributed to other, false gods. According to the accounts that pagans have left us, they believed that their gods were occupied with selfish and trivial concerns. God's priority throughout history, however, was to save a people for his glory. In Old Testament times the focus of God's plans was the covenant people, or the house of Israel, **'the one nation on earth whose God went out to redeem a people for himself, and to make a name for yourself ... by driving out nations from before your people, whom you redeemed from Egypt'** (17:21).

The building of temporal monuments seems to fall into the background when compared with the great plan to save a nation as a living testimony to God's grace. Our Lord expressed the same priorities when he told the woman of Samaria, 'Believe me, woman, a time is coming when you will worship the Father neither on this mountain nor in Jerusalem ... when the true worshippers will worship the Father in spirit and truth, for they are the kind of worshippers the Father seeks'

(John 4:21,23). Because of this David was more than willing to set aside his desire to build a temple. **'And now, Lord, let the promise you have made concerning your servant and his house be established for ever... Then men will say, "The Lord Almighty, the God over Israel, is Israel's God!" And the house of your servant will be established before you'** (17:23-24).

3. He prayed for his son (17:25-27)

Not only did David accept God's promises that a son would build a temple in David's place, but he took delight in that promise and prayed that it would indeed be so. David recognized that God knew what was for the best and prayed, 'Your will be done.' We should notice a very special feature of David's prayer in verse 25, where David confesses to God that as a result of his covenant promise, **'Your servant has found courage to pray to you.'** David now prayed with a new urgency. Of course the door to prayer had always been open to David, as we read in Psalm 102:17: 'He will respond to the prayer of the destitute; he will not despise their plea.'

Every believer knows, however, that he or she is not at all times equally inclined to come to God in prayer. There are times when we simply do not feel like praying because we do not find the courage or the heart to get on our knees before God. It is at such times that we need to be especially urgent in prayer, first of all asking God to give us a spirit of prayer. For David that spirit was stirred up by considering the covenant promises of God as they were revealed in his Word: **'You ... have revealed to your servant that you will build a house for him. So your servant has found courage to pray to you.'**

As a result of this new spirit of prayerfulness David was able to finish his prayer with assurance (17:26-27). God's promise was not just a hint of blessing to come, but a sign that

God had already begun to bless his people. It is enough for God to say the word, for his promise is as good as his actions (as the Roman centurion in Luke 7:6-8 understood). **'Now you have been pleased to bless the house of your servant, that it may continue for ever in your sight; for you, O Lord, have blessed** [or 'are blessing'] **it, and it will be blessed for ever.'** Already God was preparing the ground for future blessing and was stirring up the hearts of his people to pray for it. God's promises are blessings begun, for God never promises in vain and never gives blessings without first stirring the hearts of his people to seek them.

In the fulness of Christ we can see how this promise was indeed one of great blessing. Those who are in Christ are now part of David's house and subjects of the King of kings who sits upon his throne for ever. We have seen what God has done to establish his kingdom of grace, and our confidence to pray that Christ's kingdom will be extended yet further must surely be encouraged by the Messianic promises of this chapter.

14.
David's wars

Please read 1 Chronicles 18:1 - 20:8

King David was a man of war. That is how God described him
and for that reason David was not the man to build the temple
in Jerusalem (22:8; 28:3). This did not diminish the importance of David's career as a military commander. After all, this
was how God had called David to serve him and **'The Lord
gave David victory'** over his enemies (18:13). His son Solomon was not a better man simply because he served the Lord
during a time of peace. It was Solomon's privilege to complete
the work that David had started and, as we shall see, the peace,
stability and prosperity that were so necessary for Solomon's
work were the results of David's victories.

What, then, can we learn from the struggles and victories
of King David? Some have asked whether we can we learn
anything positive from this man of war, who lived in an age
very different from our own and at a different stage in God's
dealings with his people. God's church is no longer contained
within the nation of Israel, with its own political structures
and armies to fight against invading enemies. Today, 'We do
not wage war as the world does. The weapons we fight with
are not the weapons of the world' (2 Cor. 10:3-4) and
Christians are not to respond to personal insults with violence
(Matt. 5:39).

As we study these chapters we must always remember that David was the Lord's anointed and that it was the Lord who gave him victory over his enemies. It was God who established David's kingdom. While God's kingdom today is no longer limited to one national group centred in Jerusalem and our enemies are not Philistine armies, we need to remember that we are still subjects of a King whom God has anointed. Our King is the Lord Jesus Christ, the King of kings, and it is often in the midst of conflict and tribulation that God exalts his kingdom over his enemies (Ps. 2:6-9; Acts 14:22). David's life teaches us lessons about his honour, his victory and how others are to join in his service.

Various enemies (18:1-13)

Without going into much detail about the conflicts in which David engaged, these verses describe the victory David had over enemies on all sides. The Philistines (18:1) attacked from the coastal plain of the south-west; the Moabites (18:2) and the Edomites (18:12-13) attacked from beyond the Jordan on the south-east; and the various Aramean factions (18:3-11) were based in Syria to the north-east. The Chronicler does not dwell on the threat that they presented to the Israelite kingdom, but on the fact that God gave David victory over all his enemies and thus provided security for his people. The last words of 18:6 and 18:13 are the key text of this section: **'The Lord gave David victory everywhere he went.'**

Most attention in these verses is given to the attack of Hadadezer, King of Zobah (to the east of Hamath in Syria, a kingdom that at its zenith stretched as far as the Euphrates river), who was allied with the Syrian kingdom of Damascus. David's defeat of these powerful armies (described in 18:4)

sent shock waves throughout the region and frightened potential enemies into submission. King Tou of Hamath (another
Syrian principality) became a willing vassal of David rather
than suffer defeat, and sent his son with tribute. Verse 11 notes
the spiritual significance of these victories: they enabled
David to make material provision for the Lord's work. **'King
David dedicated these articles to the Lord, as he had done
with the silver and gold he had taken from all these
nations: Edom and Moab, the Ammonites and the
Philistines, and Amalek.'** The spoils of war did not find their
way into David's personal wealth, but were put into the
treasuries of the Lord. From the treasuries that David built up
in this way came the resources needed to build the temple.
Such a spirit of generosity is what our Lord commended in his
parable of the talents in Matthew 25:14-30, for every gift that
God gives us (whether spiritual or material) is to be dedicated
to his service and glory

Internal reorganization (18:14-17)

These verses give us a glimpse into the administrative system
that David established in Israel. From these internal reforms
initiated by David we see that he was more than just a military
commander: he was also a leader skilled in the intricate art of
statecraft. As his kingdom grew, so did the need for a central-
ized and efficient administration. In these verses the Chronicler lists the names of those who filled the most senior offices
of state. Joab, the king's nephew, was in charge of the army.
His tactical skill, shown in chapter 19, demonstrates that
David's choice was not motivated by simple nepotism. The
Kerethites and Pelethites were a closely knit personal bodyguard under the command of the courageous and loyal
Benaiah (18:17, cf. 11:22-25).

The civil administration was overseen by Jehoshaphat (18:15), whose post as recorder may have involved judicial responsibilities, for his name means, 'The Lord is Judge.' Shavsha, whose name may indicate that he was of Egyptian origin, was appointed secretary (18:16). Apart from the similar lists in 2 Samuel 8:15-18; 20:23-26 and 1 Kings 4:1-6, neither of these men is mentioned again in Scripture.

The Ammonites (19:1 - 20:3)

Only in this section does the Chronicler give us details of one of David's foreign wars. He explains how a conflict developed with Hanun, King of Ammon, and outlines the campaign that ensued. Hanun's father Nahash was a long-serving ruler of the Ammonites, with his capital at Rabbah (modern Amman, in Jordan). Although he had clashed with Saul (1 Sam. 11:1-11), he had always been on good terms with David and for that reason David sent messengers to pay his respects to Hanun upon his accession to the throne after the death of Nahash. Hanun was either a very insecure individual, or very badly advised, or both (19:3), for he responded to David's gesture of goodwill by shamefully treating David's ambassadors.

The obscene behaviour described in 19:4 was a calculated insult to David and to Israel. By shaving off these men's beards he treated them like little boys, for a full-grown beard was a sign of manhood. Making a public display of their nakedness was even worse. In Isaiah 20:3-4 this is the scenario that the prophet used to describe the shame that would be experienced by those nations which had harshly treated God's people and whom God had punished by sending them into slavery. Hanun's crude insult had political overtones for it was a challenge to David to prove that he was able to defend those who looked to him for protection. If David overlooked this gesture his ability to defend the security and integrity of his kingdom might well be called into question. Only after the event did Hanun stop to consider the implications of his actions (19:6) and when he did he took fright. He planned to strike David before David struck him. Unable to face Israel's armies on his own, Hanun hired mercenaries from Syria (or Aram), some of them the very soldiers that David had defeated already!

In the campaign that followed the military genius of Joab was displayed to the full. Caught in the difficult situation of being sandwiched between two advancing fronts, he deployed his troops to best advantage so that reinforcements could easily be transferred from one area of battle to another. He reminded the people of the true nature of the conflict in which they were engaged: **'Be strong and let us fight bravely for our people and the cities of our God. The Lord will do what is good in his sight'** (19:13). When the battle is the Lord's we know that God's enemies can never ultimately triumph.

Hanun's defeat that day at the hands of Joab led to a collapse of his coalition and the further extension of David's kingdom (19:19). Furthermore, his army was ruined (19:17-18) and his kingdom laid waste. The opening verses of chapter 20 describe the sequel to the battle the following spring, when Joab led another army to subdue the already weakened Ammonite kingdom. Joab led the assault, while David remained in Jerusalem (cf. 2 Sam. 11:1). Joab, however, allowed David the honour of accepting the surrender of the Ammonite garrison at Rabbah (20:2; 2 Sam. 12:26-31) and there David was crowned with the Ammonite crown.

The great quantity of plunder captured from the Ammonites after the fall of Rabbah greatly increased Israel's wealth. For the first time the Chronicler describes something that was to become an important feature of national life — the gangs of forced labourers who would work on prestigious building projects such as the temple (see 2 Sam. 20:24; 1 Kings 4:6; 5:13-14). Many of the captured Ammonites were consigned **'to labour with saws and with iron picks and axes'** (20:3). This, together with the description of David wearing the valuable Ammonite crown, presents a comforting picture of David's kingdom as victorious, wealthy and secure.

The Philistines (20:4-8)

These verses do not record the narrative of a campaign against the Philistines, but a series of clashes between individuals. The Israelite heroes faced powerful opponents and acquitted themselves worthily. The account of the contest in 20:5 has proved difficult to reconcile with that given in 2 Samuel 21:19 which records that 'Elhanan son of Jaare-Oregim the Bethlehemite killed Goliath the Gittite, who had a spear with a shaft like a weaver's rod.' A possible resolution is that there was a Goliath other than the Goliath killed by David in 1 Samuel 17, and that both he and his brother Lahmi were killed by Elhanan.

The king's honour

These chapters are strategically placed in the Chronicler's account of David's life. They come just after God's covenant with him in 1 Chronicles 17 and show how God kept his promises to David. God had promised David victory over his enemies (17:8) and here we read of David not only defeating his enemies on the battlefield, but being crowned as king over them. God had also promised that he would make David's name great. Although Hanun tried to humiliate him, the result of these wars was that David's reputation was enhanced. Throughout the region there was no one who dared to stand against David, for it was known that 'The Lord gave David victory everywhere he went.'

God had promised these victories to David so that his people might live in peace and be free to serve the Lord their God: 'And I will ... plant them so that they can have a home of their own and no longer be disturbed' (17:9). As a result of David's victories Israelite garrisons subdued their neighbours (18:6) and these nations brought tribute to David (18:6-8,10; 19:19). God was bringing about the peace that Solomon would later enjoy.

The highlight of God's covenant with David was that his son would build a house for the Lord as David had sought: 'When your days are over and you go to be with your fathers, I will raise up your offspring to succeed you... He is the one who will build a house for me' (17:11-12). David's role as a man of war prevented him from building the temple, but even his military victories played an important part in the preparation for that work. When the defeated Arameans and the new-found ally in Tou, King of Hamath, brought their treasure to David (18:7-11), he could have used these riches for himself. Instead of doing that he **'dedicated these articles to the Lord'**, and so built up a fund that his son would later use to build the temple.

These verses help us to wrestle with two questions that often perplex God's people: why does God bring disappointments into the lives of his people, and why does he allow enemies to harass them? The book of Job teaches us that there are no easy answers to these questions, but we can take courage from David's example in these chapters. He was frustrated in his desire to build the temple, because he was called upon to fight for his country on the battlefield. But the very warfare that disqualified him from building the temple helped to provide the gold and silver with which the temple was built. David must have been vexed at having to face the constant hostility of his enemies, yet the victories which arose out of these conflicts were what made him such a mighty servant of God. The spoils of war enabled Solomon to do that work that was so close to David's heart — build the temple.

Jonathan Edwards recorded in his diary that he would seek to 'improve afflictions to the uttermost'. In other words, he would seek to see how God was working for good in the very things that troubled him most. David's wars are an example of how we can do just that. In the midst of severe tribulation David's royal honour was established for ever.

The king's enemies

A diverse and daunting array of enemies was drawn up against David. There were *old* enemies, for the Philistines had been a long-standing thorn in the flesh of the Israelites. The Rephaites were a fearful race of giants that had lived in Canaan at least since the time of Abraham. They had struck terror into the Israelites when they returned to occupy the promised land (see Gen. 15:20; Deut. 3:11,13). In 20:4 we find one of their descendants fighting alongside the Philistines. When evil is not thoroughly purged from our lives it has a tendency to return and trouble us later.

There were *treacherous* enemies. Hanun, King of the Ammonites, was a prime example of this. He was a disturbed and paranoid individual who was suspicious of David's generosity and reacted in an irrational way. It should come as no surprise that wicked men should behave like that, because the very nature of sin is 'lawlessness' (1 John 3:4). The powers of evil do not conform to the right ways of God by which we seek to govern our lives, and as a result their actions are thoroughly unpredictable. The believer needs to recognize this if he is to be on his guard against his enemy Satan, who is compared to a roaring lion, seeking any way to devour God's people (1 Peter 5:8).

There were *strong* enemies gathered against David. The Chronicler records the strength of Hanun's mercenary force in 19:7 and the giant Philistines of 20:5-6. Taken together these enemies were a mighty force to be reckoned with. Yet without exception they were defeated — even the mighty Philistines **'fell at the hands of David and his men'** (20:8). Who can stand against the Lord's anointed?

The same is true of God's enemies in every age. The Lord's anointed will always face organized opposition. Psalm 2:2 describes how 'The kings of the earth take their stand and the rulers gather together against the Lord and against his Anointed One.' The very work of God to establish his kingdom provokes his enemies to fight against it (Matt. 13:24-25; 2 Tim. 3:12; Rev. 12:11-12). But these enemies are in the very process of being defeated (1 Cor. 15:23-26). They will go the same way as the Philistines, Arameans, Ammonites and Rephaites.

> Therefore, you kings, be wise,
>   be warned, you rulers of the earth.
> Serve the Lord with fear
>   and rejoice with trembling.
> Kiss the Son, lest he be angry
>   and you be destroyed in your way,
> for his wrath can flare up in a moment.
>   Blessed are all who take refuge in him
>
>   (Ps. 2:10-12).

The fact that believers are members of God's kingdom of grace does not mean that they will be without enemies. Quite the contrary! There was a time when we were God's enemies and at peace with the world. Now the position is reversed. As well as having new friends we now have new enemies. These may be people who used to be our friends while we were strangers to God's grace. They may be our colleagues at work, perhaps even members of our own families. Now they resent the changes that God's grace has wrought in our lives. In fact Jesus said, 'In this world you will have trouble' (John 16:33). This trouble may come from old, cunning or strong enemies, but we need not be afraid, for in Christ we can overcome them all (Phil. 4:13).

The king's servants

While David was at the centre of attention all through these chapters, he was not always at the centre of the action. Especially in chapter 19 we noted that Joab took the lead in defeating the Ammonite coalition. In fact the individual contributions of a whole array of David's servants are mentioned in this section (18:12-17; 19:10-15; 20:1,4-7). Without their enthusiastic participation in the life of the nation, David's kingdom would have crumbled. There was a high degree of delegation and co-operation in David's kingdom.

David was not like the marshall of the French armies at the battle of Oudenarde in 1708, the Duke of Vendôme. Reports of the battle describe how Vendôme fought with the courage of a lion, but he could not delegate, he would not take advice and always insisted on being in the heat of the battle to gauge the situation for himself. As a result the French army suffered a great defeat for want of strategic leadership to direct the resources where they were most needed. Although David was the Lord's anointed he was not to be a king without a people. He was supported and served by a willing people — whose gifts were given opportunity to develop with use.

This is a biblical principle that goes back at least to Moses in Exodus 18:17-23. In the New Testament Paul describes the church as a body of which Christ is the Head, but the body is held together and built up only 'as each part does its work' (Eph. 4:16). There is no place among God's people for those who do not want to play their part in the king's work.

Among David's servants some unexpected names are included, for even his enemies became his subjects. Some resisted his authority until the end and were brought into slavery. Among these were the citizens of Rabbah, who were consigned 'to labour with saws and with iron picks and axes' (20:3). Others, however, came willingly into David's service. Among these were the Kerethites and Pelethites (18:17), who were recruited from among the Philistines and Phoenicians to provide David with a palace guard. They were fiercely loyal to David, even when most of the nation supported Absalom, and they seem to have been disbanded only after David's death.

While there are many today who flaunt their hostility to King Jesus, the New Testament teaches us of a day when 'At the name of Jesus every knee [shall] bow' (Phil. 2:9-10; 1 Cor. 15:24-27). This truth presents a sobering challenge to us all. Some, of course, will bow willingly and will consider it the greatest of privileges to serve Christ. Others, however, will refuse to submit to the gospel of Jesus Christ. Throughout their lives on this earth they will resist him at every turn, but the day will come when they will bow before him and will be placed under his yoke throughout eternity. This yoke will not be light or easy, but a terrible torment. How will you serve the King of kings in eternity? Serve him you must! How are you serving him now?

15.
David's census

Please read 1 Chronicles 21:1-30

This chapter records a dark and mysterious incident in the history of David's life, and in doing so corrects a misapprehension that some people have about the book of Chronicles. It has been argued that the Chronicler gives us an idealized picture of David, editing out the unflattering incidents in his life and concentrating on those that present him in a favourable light. This line of argument misrepresents the Chronicler's work, for he passes over aspects of David's life that are both good and bad. Although the Chronicler does not recount the story of David's sin with Bathsheba, as does the author of 2 Samuel, the record of the unauthorized census clearly shows that David had feet of clay. We weep for David as we read this chapter. Indeed in this account of the census and the plague that resulted from it we see with almost painful clarity the malevolent influence of Satan and the depth of sinful depravity in the life of David.

David was, like the rest of the Israelites, a sinner who needed forgiveness and reconciliation with God. In fact his exalted status made his sins more serious, and emphasized his need for God's mercy. That is made abundantly clear in this chapter. But, on a more positive note, God's provision for sinners is also emphasized as the narrative unfolds. The focus of the Chronicler's history is the ministry of the temple and consequently the events that he chose to record are those which highlight the importance of the temple as a place to which sinners must go for forgiveness. In chapter 17 God had indicated that a temple would be built by David's son. Now in this passage God showed where that temple would be built — on the place where David offered his sacrifice to turn back God's wrath from his kingdom (22:1).

David brought disaster on his people (21:1-7)

After the blessings that David had enjoyed and the spiritual maturity that he had displayed we are at a loss to understand how he could have fallen into such serious sin. It is sometimes hard for us to understand how Christians can fall so quickly and so deeply into sin. We need constantly to be aware of the strength of the forces of darkness arrayed against us. Before we consider the forces that influenced David's behaviour in ordering a census of Israel's fighting men, we must look at what he did and why his actions were sinful.

David failed to appreciate the significance of what he was doing when he ordered Joab and the commanders of his troops, **'Go and count the Israelites from Beersheba to Dan'** (21:2). In the modern world we are used to a wide range of surveys and censuses being held as researchers try to discover the needs and demands of the population at large. In ancient Israel, however, censuses were not just head counts to guide public policy, for they had a profound spiritual significance.

It was God's prerogative to order a census of his people, and he tended to do so only on landmark occasions in their history. For example, a census was ordered just after the Exodus of the Israelites from Egypt and the giving of the law at Mount Sinai (see Num. 1:2; 4:2,22) and again forty years later when the Israelites arrived at the borders of the promised land (see Num. 26:2,4). By comparing the results of these two censuses we can see how wonderfully God preserved and blessed his people during their period of wandering in the wilderness. God's particular concern for the full number of his elect can be seen in his order that each member of his covenant people should be counted and recorded. As well as demonstrating the precision of God's love this also emphasized God's ownership of his people and his desire that they be ready for his service. It is significant to notice in this respect the purpose of the censuses recorded in Numbers, which was to record those 'who are able to serve in the army' (Num. 1:3; 26:2).

Censuses in Israel were also God's appointed way of raising the resources needed to build and sustain a place of sacrifice in the midst of the people. They were associated with a kind of spiritual poll tax. This was the case when the tabernacle was built in the time of Moses (see Exod. 38:25) and when the temple was repaired in the time of Joash (2 Kings 12:4). In Exodus 30:11-16 Moses received a detailed set of regulations that were to govern the administration of censuses in Israel. Each person counted in a census was to pay a *copher*, or 'ransom for his life'. (This word is derived from the Hebrew verb *caphar*, 'to cover', which is one of the richest theological themes in the whole Old Testament.) When the Israelite paid this sum of money he was recognizing that his life belonged to the Lord (not to the king or any other man) and that he needed God's provision of sacrifice to purge away the guilt of his sin.

This payment amounted to half a shekel and became known as the 'half-shekel tax', or simply the 'temple tax'. Although as the Son of God the Lord Jesus was under no obligation to pay it, this is the tax that Jesus paid on behalf of Peter and himself in Matthew 17:24-27. In Exodus 30:16 this payment of half a shekel was called 'atonement money' and was used 'for the service of the Tent of Meeting'. Its lasting significance was that it reminded the people that Jehovah was their King and their lives belonged to him, and that his greatest priority for them was the atonement provided by the shedding of blood.

When David ordered his census in 21:1 his thinking does not appear to have been influenced by these concerns. There is no evidence that divine guidance influenced his decision, nor is there evidence of any compelling purpose arising from the outworking of God's providence that would call for the numbering of God's people. Furthermore, it would appear that the census was not conducted according to the regulations laid down in Exodus 30:11-16, as there is no evidence that the atonement money was collected. Although the passage does not explicitly describe what influenced David to order the census as he did, most commentators agree that his motive was at the heart of the problem — and we shall return to this consideration later.

To summarize, it was the combination of a lack of divine warrant, failure to follow God's law and a wrong motive that made David's actions so sinful. They were clearly sinful, even to Joab, who asked, **'Why does my lord want to do this? Why should he bring guilt** *[ashmah]* **on Israel?'** (21:3). *Ashmah* is a word describing disobedience that must be atoned for. God's anger must surely manifest itself in the plague of which Exodus 30:12 warned. That was ominously evident to Joab! So too was the need for God's anger to be turned back by the atonement of blood which would be made in 21:26.

Now let us consider why David did this evil thing. God's people are caught up in spiritual battles that are often far bigger than they imagine as they look from their earthly vantage-point. In Luke 22:31-32 Jesus gave Simon Peter a brief insight into the spiritual conflict that would soon engulf the struggling disciple. In these verses we get a similar insight into the forces influencing David. Let us look at his sin from three angles.

1. Satan's angle (21:1)

Satan was the agitator behind David's sin: **'Satan rose up against Israel and incited David...'** Satan hates God and resents the love he lavishes upon his people. Constantly he seeks to drive a wedge of suspicion between believers and their Redeemer. His name means 'accuser' and his other title, 'the devil', means 'the slanderer'. In Job 1:6-12 and 2:1-7 we read how Satan tried to blacken Job's good name (see also Zech. 3 for Satan's assault upon Joshua the high priest).

In this passage we read of Satan acting as an *agent provocateur*. In the garden of Eden the serpent acted in such a way, seeking to instigate the sin that alienated God from men and turned men away from God. The Bible does not tell us very much to explain the origin of evil, although the description of the Prince of Tyre in Ezekiel 28 becomes a figurative description of Lucifer, the prince of the morning. He was created perfect and dwelt with God until 'wickedness was found' in him (Ezek. 28:15). As a result he was cast from God's presence and from that time forth he devoted himself to frustrating God's plans and corrupting his creation. We must flee from every temptation he sets before us!

2. David's angle (21:2)

Unfortunately David did not resist Satan. Instead he listened to the devil and followed his advice. The idea of taking a census of the fighting men of Israel was innocent enough in itself, for God had ordered something similar in Exodus 38:25

and Numbers 1:2; 26:2. The census that David ordered, however, took no account of God's will, for he did not consult with anyone nor did he seek God's guidance.

This census had much more to do with David's pride and self-congratulation than the will of God. Success had begun to go to David's head. The blessing that he had enjoyed, and especially the victories described in chapters 18-20, began to deceive him. God's covenant with Abraham included the promise that his descendants would be as numerous as the stars in the sky and the sand on the seashore — in other words, so numerous that they could not be counted (see Gen. 15:5; 22:17). Solomon acknowledged how faithful God had been to his promise (1 Kings 3:8). In the context of another census David acknowledged this promise to Israel (27:23), but in this instance he forgot just how richly God fulfils his promises. David himself had written, 'Some trust in chariots and some in horses, but we trust in the name of the Lord our God' (Ps. 20:7). Now he was beginning to glory in the very things that were only the symptoms of blessing, not the causes of it. He looked to static and predictable human resources, rather than to the dynamic and direct intervention of the sovereign Lord.

David also began to despise the counsel of his advisers. Joab was a hard-headed military man who was used to making the calculations that generals have to make on the basis of numbers, but even he could see the foolishness of David's command in verse 2. His reply was respectful but to the point: **'May the Lord multiply his troops a hundred times over. My lord the king, are they not all my lord's subjects? Why does my lord want to do this? Why should he bring guilt on Israel?'** (21:3). So serious were Joab's reservations that he could not bring himself to comply fully with the king's instructions (21:6). Perhaps Joab's omission of the tribe of Levi from the census referred back to Numbers 1:47-49, and it has been suggested that his failure to count the Benjamites was because the Lord's intervention in judgement prevented it.

David pressed on with his plans. The malevolent influence of Satan has been mentioned already, but the devil could not have influenced David if the king had not been willing to collaborate. David could not evade responsibility for his actions by shifting the blame onto Satan. Adam sought to do that after he ate the forbidden fruit by pointing to Eve and saying, 'The woman you put here with me — she gave me some fruit from the tree, and I ate it' (Gen. 3:12). David could not shift the blame for his actions to God, whose law he had flouted, nor to his advisers, whose counsel he had ignored. Neither can we evade the guilt of our sins, for we are responsible creatures who must answer for our actions before God.

3. God's angle

We should not imagine that God was powerless in this exchange between Satan and David. Even in the midst of David's sinful behaviour God was working out his plans. See the parallel account in 2 Samuel 24:1: 'The anger of the Lord burned against Israel, and he incited David against them, saying, "Go and take a census of Israel and Judah."' This is not a contradiction of the Chronicler's account. Neither does it teach that God is the cause of evil, or that David's guilt was any less because of God's hand in the matter. The Scriptures teach that God is sovereign over all his creatures and all their actions, even when those actions are sinful. Yet God is never the cause of evil and can never be tainted by the defilement of his creatures' sins. An example is provided by Adam's first sin. This sin and its terrible consequences were part of God's sovereign decree (Rom. 8:20), yet Adam rightly bore the responsibility for his actions (see also Luke 22:22; James 1:13-14).

David cast himself upon God's mercy (21:8-15)

Even before God challenged David, his conscience convicted him of his wrongdoing. Very serious expressions are used in this passage to describe David's sin. It is described as **'repulsive'** (21:6) and **'evil'** (21:7), and David hmself said to God, **'I have sinned greatly by doing this... I have done a very foolish thing'** (21:8). As a result disaster struck David's kingdom, when God sent out a destroying angel to strike the land with plague for three days (21:14-16).

The angel mentioned in these verses is to be distinguished from the angel of the Lord who appeared to Abraham, Joshua, Gideon and to Samson's parents. That angel was worshipped as Lord and was an Old Testament appearance of the Second Person of the Trinity. The destroying angel mentioned in these verses was most probably one of the many heavenly angels. He was a messenger bringing a message of death, like the angel of death that went amongst the Egyptians on the night God took Israel out of Egypt (Exod. 12). We should not think of this angel as being evil in himself, but having a ministry of destruction.

It must have been shocking for God's people to think that such an angel should visit Israel, yet this was the consequence of David's sin. The sins of God's people are no less serious than the sins of others, and we should never allow ourselves to think otherwise. Every sin demands the payment of an infinite price and the only reason why that price is not extracted from believers is because another has paid it on their behalf. When God's people become careless about sin God has to chasten them with bitter sorrow. Yet even when he chastises them sorely, as he did in this case, he gives them evidences of his mercy. That was most surely David's experience.

1. God allowed David to select his own punishment (21:9-12)

In ancient Greece a condemned man was sometimes allowed to choose his method of punishment. This was an option which tested a person's character as he faced death. The three options set before David — three years of famine, three months of invasion, or three days of plague — were a test of his faith in God. Famine would have placed his people at the mercy of foreign merchants who would supply his kingdom with imported grain. Invasion would have placed them at the mercy of people as unpredictable as Hanun, King of the Ammonites (19:2-7). The plague placed him unmistakably in the hands of the Lord, for the destroying angel went out from God and did his bidding.

For this reason David chose the plague. This was a courageous choice, for David knew the holy character of God. He knew that it is a dreadful thing to fall into the hands of the living God (Heb. 10:31). Especially when we have offended God and our consciences have been smitten, we find it difficult to draw near to God, for we know what our sins rightly deserve. Yet David showed great confidence in the constancy of God, because he would rather fall into the hands of the Judge of all the earth, who will do what is right, than into the hands of vindictive and unpredictable men. David knew that God is merciful and, while he would chastise him for a time, he would not remain angry for ever.

2. God was grieved at his people's suffering (21:15)

A dramatic turning-point in David's fortunes is described in this verse. This is attributed to God's mercy for his people because he **'was grieved because of the calamity'**. God's grief is not an acknowledgement that he has done any wrong and now regrets his actions. God's actions are always without fault. As a Father he is neither too strict nor too lenient; in everything he maintains a perfect balance. There is no part of the lives of his people that he would arrange differently if he had the opportunity, so the grief referred to here is not the same as that which we often experience when we consider the consequences of our actions.

The lesson this narrative teaches is that even when God chastens us he never ceases to be merciful. God's mercy is like the sun, which may be hidden from our view when rain-clouds fill the sky. These clouds come to fulfil a very important task, but when enough rain has fallen the clouds clear away and we feel the sun's warmth again. When the sun returns we know that it has been behind the clouds all the time. Our experiences of God's chastening are rather like the showers that blot out the sun's light and warmth. They come for our own good and when God has taught us the lessons we needed to learn he takes them away so that we can enjoy the warmth of his fellowship again.

It was important for David to learn the lesson that he learned in this chapter. There was no other way for God to teach him but in this hard way. Now that David had learnt his lesson, God's anger was spent and his mercy clearly reasserted itself. God's way of dealing with his people may not always be pleasant in the short term, but it is always merciful. He teaches us to cast ourselves on God's mercy and to pray, 'In wrath remember mercy' (Hab. 3:2).

David discovered God's provision for sinners (21:16-30)

In verse 8 David made a demanding request of the Lord after his sin: 'Now, I beg you, take away the guilt of your servant.' As the destroying angel hovered between heaven and earth

David's prayer changed. He did not pray for himself, but for his people: **'Was it not I who ordered the fighting men to be counted? I am the one who has sinned and done wrong. These are but sheep. What have they done? O Lord my God, let your hand fall upon me and my family, but do not let this plague remain on your people'** (21:17). Moses had made a similar offer after the children of Israel sinned at Mount Sinai (Exod. 32:32). Now David offered to die in the place of his people, and to suffer for his own sins. What David did not realize was that, while his offer was well-intentioned, it was wholly inadequate.

> No man can redeem the life of another
>   or give to God a ransom for him—
> the ransom for a life is costly,
>   no payment is ever enough—
> that he should live on for ever
>   and not see decay
>
> (Ps. 49:7-9).

The prospect for David and the Israelites was not as bleak as it would at first appear. Although divine justice unleashed the destroying angel to punish sin, from verse 18 onwards the Lord set out the provision that he has made for extending mercy to sinners. The angel who brought destruction also brought a message of salvation to David through the prophet Gad. David was to go to the place where the destroying angel was hovering overlooking Jerusalem and follow very closely the instructions that he was given (21:18-19). There he was to offer a sacrifice for his sin.

1. A costly sacrifice (21:20-26)

This is emphasized by the bargain struck between David and Araunah (or Ornan according to the Hebrew text). Araunah owned the site where David was to offer a sacrifice and the oxen and wood that David was to use for the sacrifice. When David offered to buy them Araunah refused to accept payment, but David insisted upon paying a proper price and the sizeable sum of 600 shekels was paid for the site, and presumably the oxen and fuel as well (21:25).

David's explanation was: **'No, I insist on paying the full price. I will not ... sacrifice a burnt offering that costs me nothing'** (21:24). This willingness to make a costly sacrifice is often applied as a challenge to the Christian worshipper, and rightly so. The primary reference, however, is to the one who would ransom a sinner from God's condemnation. This called for a very costly sacrifice. When the Old Testament worshipper came to the temple God expected the very best animals from his flock to be offered on the altar. When it came to the ultimate sacrifice only the most costly sacrifice could purchase everlasting salvation. God the Father gave no less a treasure than his only-begotten Son (John 3:16; Rom. 8:32) and our Lord willingly gave his life (John 15:13) because he loved his people to the end, even though that cost him indescribable torment. No other price could save sinners.

2. A blood sacrifice (21:26,28)

'David built an altar to the Lord there and sacrificed burnt offerings and fellowship offerings' (21:26). David could not offer himself as a sacrifice to pay the debt of his own sins or those of his people, but God would accept a substitute — the sacrificial animal. When the blood of the victim was shed the lives of the people could be spared. That was God's way, throughout the Old Testament, of pointing to the death of his Son. Only his precious blood could pay the debt of sin and appease God's anger.

The effect of the blood sacrifice was described in the symbolic action of 21:27: **'Then the Lord spoke to the angel, and he put his sword back into his sheath.'** The sword is a picture of God's anger unleashed in judgement, and only the shedding of blood could prevent that sword from taking its toll on the people of Jerusalem. Yet the blood of the sacrifice sheathed the sword. This is an excellent illustration of the often overlooked Bible word 'propitiation' used in Romans 3:25 and 1 John 4:10. God needs to be propitiated because he is rightly angry with sinners on account of their sins. There is only one thing that can appease God's anger and that is a blood sacrifice.

We should never think that we can be saved from the punishment due to our sins just because God is merciful in his character. If God's mercy alone could save sinners, then there would have been no reason for God to establish the Old Testament system of blood sacrifice. Even more importantly, there would have been no reason for God to give his Son to die on the cross. Unless we come directly to the cross and acknowledge our debt to God and ask him to accept the blood shed on the cross as the payment of our debt, then God's mercy will be of no benefit to us. It is the blood of Christ that sheathes the sword of his anger and enables God to offer mercy with justice.

3. An accepted sacrifice (21:26,28)

'David saw that the Lord had answered him on the threshing-floor of Araunah the Jebusite' (21:28). The sacrifice that the Lord provided for our salvation is the only sacrifice that God will accept. Not every sacrifice offered to God is acceptable to him. Yet there was a very clear indication that David's sacrifice was accepted as a ransom for Jerusalem because **'The Lord answered ... with fire from heaven'** (21:26). This calls to mind the endorsement given to Elijah's sacrifice on Mount Carmel. In contrast to the prophets of Baal, God listened to Elijah and consumed his offering with fire from heaven (1 Kings 18:22-24,36-39).

As Christians we have been given a sign from heaven that our trust in the cross of Christ is well founded, and that sign is the resurrection of Jesus. The resurrection set the seal of the Father's approval upon his Son's finished work. Paul tells us that he 'was delivered over to death for our sins and was raised to life for our justification' (Rom. 4:25), and that 'We know that the one who raised the Lord Jesus from the dead will also raise us with Jesus and present us with you in his presence' (2 Cor. 4:14).

Conclusion

David learned about the greatness of God's mercies, but he also learned that free forgiveness does not remove all the scars of our sins, for we continue to bear some of those for the rest of our earthly lives. Even though David brought an accepted sacrifice and saw the sword in the angel's hand being put away, he carried the shame of his disobedience for some time to come afterwards. **'David could not go ... to enquire of God, because he was afraid of the sword of the angel of the Lord'** (21:30). This is rather like the shame we feel when we have hurt a friend, even though we have apologized and our apology has been accepted. This feature of our still imperfect lives on earth does not deny the mercy of God or the atonement he has made for his people, but it reminds us that even forgiven sin can cause shame.

That is why we must always insist on high standards of conduct in our daily lives. Paul answered those who believed that free grace made holiness a matter of indifference to believers, by urging them: 'Offer yourselves to God, as those who have been brought from death to life; and offer the parts of your body to him as instruments of righteousness.' He asked these believers to look back at their past sins and ask themselves, 'What benefit did you reap at that time from the things you are now ashamed of? Those things result in death!' (Rom. 6:13,21). The lives we offer as living sacrifices to God greatly affect our enjoyment of God's grace. We should seek to offer lives that have been sanctified by costly sacrifice, not lives that have cost us nothing.

16.
A father's words

Please read 1 Chronicles 22:1-19

The temple that Solomon built in Jerusalem is the centrepiece of the book of Chronicles. In the Chronicler's own day it was the symbol of national identity for the Jews who returned from exile, but the Chronicler wanted it to be more than that. For him it was the point of reference for Israel's knowledge of God. The temple was a symbol both of God's holiness and of his grace, and its construction dominated the history of his people. King David had sensed the urgency of this work in his lifetime. It had been his longing to build the temple himself, but when the Lord prevented him he devoted himself to making preparations for Solomon's work. In the final section of 1 Chronicles (from chapter 22 onwards) there is a mounting air of expectancy as each chapter in some way prepares the way for the great work that would commence when David died.

When we plan to build a new house it is exciting to imagine what it might be like. Our dream house may include many things that never materialize. Some of them prove to be too expensive, or are simply impracticable. However, when a plot of ground is bought and the builder lays out the site and the bills start coming in, then the project is no longer a dream, but a visible reality — and the cost has to be counted. In this chapter the Chronicler notes two developments that emphasize the reality of God's plans to build a temple in Jerusalem:

a *construction site* has been designated and *material provision* has been made.

The significance of Araunah's threshing-floor (22:1)

The threshing-floor that David had bought from Araunah in 21:24-25 was initially to offer a sacrifice to appease God's anger as it hung over Jerusalem as a result of David's unauthorized census. There were other uses that God had in mind for that site, for God planned the tragic events of chapter 21 to mark out the place where his people would build the temple in which sacrifices would be offered to him. Many years earlier God had promised that such a place would be shown to them and to this place all the tribes would come to bring their sacrifices.

Until David made the offering on the site of Araunah's threshing-floor God had not shown his people where that place ought to be. Exactly *how* God made it clear to David that Araunah's threshing-floor was to be the site of the temple is not recorded, but that conclusion is clearly recorded in 22:1: **'Then David said, "The house of the Lord God is to be here, and also the altar of burnt offering for Israel."'**

God had directed David to a site of great historical significance. In 2 Chronicles 3:1 we are told that this site was on Mount Moriah, the mountain to which Abraham had been sent by God to offer his son Isaac. In Genesis 22 we read of that sorrowful journey made by Abraham and Isaac, and the willingness of the father to sacrifice his greatly loved son. We also read of how God spared Isaac and provided a ram to die in his place. In that action there was a prophecy, for Abraham called the place 'Jehovah Jireh' or, 'The Lord Will Provide,' for 'On the mountain of the Lord it will be provided' (Gen. 22:14).

The whole of biblical history leads up to the day when God made his great provision for sinners on a hill overlooking Jerusalem. He gave the only begotten Son whom he had loved from all eternity as a sacrificial gift. There was no ram on Calvary to take the place of Jesus when he died on the cross because he was the substitute for sinners — 'the Lamb of God, who takes away the sins of the world'. This hillside outside Jerusalem where the destroying angel was turned back was to become the place where daily sacrifices would be offered for the people, and this would be an ongoing pointer to the day when animals would need to be sacrificed no longer.

David's legacy for Solomon (22:2-5,12-16)

The most obvious legacy that David left Solomon was the *daunting task* of building a house for the Lord. David did not minimize what would be involved: **'The house to be built for the Lord should be of great magnificence and fame and splendour in the sight of all the nations'** (22:5). This temple was to be the visible symbol of God's presence on earth and must be worthy of the one who rules both heaven and earth. Such a God deserves nothing less than the best that our hands can offer him, so the temple was to be the very best that human craftsmanship could produce. Excellence and thoroughness ought to mark everything we do for God.

David was also conscious of Solomon's weaknesses when he spoke of this daunting responsibility. Like most parents David loved his son, but unlike some parents his love was not naïve. Some parents cannot imagine that their children could possibly do any wrong. If there is trouble it must have been caused by someone else! Consequently they fail to guide and discipline their children properly, and as a result the children suffer. David had many sons, and loved them all — even the wayward Absalom (2 Sam. 18:33). Through bitter experience, however, David had learned to assess the strengths and weaknesses of those he loved. Each son was an individual and had his own strengths and weaknesses.

Solomon was **'young and inexperienced'** and David made special mention of that fact (22:5). David was not minimizing Solomon's potential as a leader — simply noting that his gifts were untested and undeveloped. There were many mistakes he would make and many lessons he would learn, but these all lay ahead of him. Just then Solomon needed direction and prompting and that is what David sought to give him (see 22:5,11-13).

Another legacy that David left Solomon was *material provision*. Building the temple was going to be an immensely costly work, and to ease the burden on Solomon's shoulders David had started gathering together the resources that he would need. The contents of that fund are summarized in verses 2-4 and 14-16: there were skilled workmen (22:2,15-16), large amounts of metals, both precious and non-precious (22:3,14) and the finest timber from Lebanon (22:4).

It is the instinctive desire of most parents to provide for their children so that they might give them the best possible start in life. That is a worthy desire for a believer to have, for while we know that the Lord will provide for our daily needs, he also expects us to make prudent provision: 'Houses and wealth are inherited from parents' (Prov. 19:14); 'Children should not have to save up for their parents, but parents for their children' (2 Cor. 12:14). David's desire to help Solomon had the added incentive that the materials he gathered would be used in the Lord's service. Yet he knew that material provision alone was not sufficient.

The most important legacy that David left to his son was *spiritual instruction*. All the building materials that David had laid up would have been wasted if Solomon's heart and life were not dedicated to the Lord. Without a spiritual approach to his work, Solomon could never magnify the Lord, no matter how competently he built the temple edifice. In verses 11-13 David set before Solomon some truths of great importance.

There was a prayer for blessing: **'Now, my son, the Lord be with you, and may you have success'** (22:11). Indeed, there can be no real success apart from God's presence. Then this message is repeated when David points Solomon to God's law. Solomon was later to acknowledge his great need for wisdom, but even before that David had shown him where to find it. God gave Solomon a truly exceptional gift of wisdom, but the wisdom that comes from studying and applying God's law is available to all who will pay heed to it (Ps. 19:7; 119:97-100). David prayed, **'May the Lord give you discretion and understanding when he puts you in command over Israel, so that you may keep the law of the Lord your God. Then you will have success if you are careful to observe the decrees and laws that the Lord gave to Moses for Israel'** (22:12-13).

Unfortunately we do not always appreciate the wisdom contained in God's law, at times preferring that we should be left to do as we please. Unfortunately the human conscience — even that of a believer — without the discipline of God's law is unpredictable and can lead us into foolish behaviour. One of the most frequently used Hebrew words for sin is *awon*, and this emphasizes the perversity and twistedness of the sinful human nature. This perverse trait in the characters of fallen men and women causes them to resent the restrictions that God's law places on them, so as to make it seem foolish and bothersome.

We should think of God's law as a fence that keeps us out of danger, rather than as a burden. If we were walking near a quicksand or a minefield we would be very glad of such a fence and the protection it gives. We are not aware of all the dangers that lie ahead of us in this sinful world, but God knows and in his wisdom he has guided us by giving us his law. God's law is never an outdated relic from a past age, as some imagine. Nor is it a set of rules that we can ever safely discard. The circumstances of the times in which we live may change, but the substance of our sinfulness and the temptations that we face never change. God's wisdom and his law never change. Even centuries after Moses, David saw how important it was to reassert the authority of the law that the Lord had given through his servant Moses on Mount Sinai.

There is also in David's words a *promise* of blessing. God had given a great deal to Solomon and this was the beginning of even greater blessing. God had given his law as a guide and his covenant to encourage. When Solomon made use of these means of grace by paying attention to God's law and placing his trust in God's promises he would experience blessing: **'Then you will have success if you are careful to observe the decrees and laws that the Lord gave to Moses for Israel. Be strong and courageous. Do not be afraid or discouraged'** (22:13).

David admitted his limitations (22:6-11)

These verses give David's own account of the message he had received from God in chapter 17. He had been told that the temple he had wished to build for the Lord would in fact be built by his son. In that chapter Solomon's name had not been mentioned (although it would appear from 22:9 that David knew at that time that Solomon was the favoured son). David now recounts the reasons God had given for allocating the work to Solomon: **'You have shed much blood and have fought many wars. You are not to build a house for my Name, because you have shed much blood on the earth in my sight. But you will have a son who will be a man of peace**

**and rest... He is the one who will build a house for my
Name'** (22:8-10). In these words David acknowledged that
God had put a restriction on him, and recognized God's
reasons.

This is not to say that Solomon was a more virtuous
individual than David. David was known as 'a man after God's
own heart', just as Solomon was known as Jedidiah or 'beloved of God'. When David went out to fight in battle, it was
as the Lord's anointed to deliver God's people from the
oppression of their enemies. David served the Lord as a soldier
by fighting his battles (14:10; 18:6,13; 19:13) and it was
because of David's military achievements that Solomon was
able to enjoy the peace that his name prophesied. Solomon
enjoyed his many privileges because of God's great goodness,
not because he merited them: **'And I will give him rest from
all his enemies on every side ... and I will grant Israel peace
and quiet during his reign'** (22:9).

Solomon was to serve the Lord in a different capacity from
his father, because God had equipped him for a different kind
of service. David's gifts and background did not prepare him
for a more settled work of consolidation. His service was not
inferior, only *different*. On the other hand, Solomon's peaceful upbringing after the security of the kingdom had been
established fitted him for the more contemplative task of
designing and building the temple. David had the grace to
acknowledge God's wisdom in allocating work to him and his
son, and willingly acquiesced in God's plans.

In 1 Corinthians 12:11 Paul explains how our sovereign
God shapes the lives of men and women by giving (and on
occasions even withdrawing) gifts: 'And he gives them to each
one, just as he determines.' To some God may give many gifts
to prepare them for a prominent work affecting the lives of
many people. Others are given the gifts of ministering in the
home or to individuals. Some are given the gifts of preaching

and leadership; others are able to use their hands to create beauty or their ears to listen, but in each case the service we render is regulated by the gifts we have. In each instance the service God's people render to him is of eternal value. John Milton reflected on that fact in his poem 'On his Blindness' after he lost his eyesight:

> Thousands at his bidding speed and post
>   o'er Land and Ocean without rest:
> They also serve who only stand and wait.

It is important to recognize our limitations. To rush into a work to which God has not called us, and for which he has not fitted us, is to seek disaster. Equally sinful is the refusal to recognize our gifts and to use them. The question we are to ask is not whether we have gifts from God and a service to render. We are to seek out those gifts and, whatever they might be, consecrate them to the Lord. 'Think of yourself with sober judgement, in accordance with the measure of faith God has given you... We have different gifts, according to the grace given us' (Rom. 12:3-6). Let us use them!

David instructed the nation's leaders (22:17-19)

The heavy burden of building the temple was not to fall exclusively on Solomon's shoulders. As the man who would be king, he would take the lead, but with the support and encouragement of his people. These verses describe how David challenged the nation's leaders to help Solomon (22:17). God had blessed them and their nation, and David encouraged them to acknowledge their debt to God: **'Is not the Lord your God with you? And has he not granted you rest on every side?'** (22:18). Now they were to join with Solomon

in responding to God's goodness by devoting themselves to
his service.

David gave them an insight into the work to which they
would be giving themselves.

1. Holy work

The temple was not to be a monument to the greatness of
David, or Solomon, or even the nation of Israel, but was to be
'the sanctuary of the Lord God' (22:19). It was to be a holy
place set aside from ordinary affairs to contain **'the ark of the
covenant of the Lord and the sacred articles belonging to
God'**. This work must be done in a godly way, with godly
motives and to the glory of God.

2. Hard work

At the end of verse 16 David finished his advice to Solomon
with the challenge: 'Now begin the work.' That challenge is
now repeated to the nation's leaders as he tells them, **'Begin
to build'** (22:19). In both verses the Hebrew verb means 'to
stand up' or 'to brace yourself for hard work'. The Lord's work
is not done in an armchair, or in a laid-back posture, but with
our feet planted firmly on the ground, our sleeves rolled up and
the resolve to approach our task with vigour.

3. Heart work

David would later call upon his people to contribute generously from their material wealth towards the building of the
temple, but even more important than this generosity was the
commitment of their hearts: **'Now devote your heart and
soul to seeking the Lord your God'** (22:19). After all, the
temple was to be a place where God's people would seek the

Lord (see 2 Chron. 7:14). If the temple was to be more than a mere monument to a human king it had to be built by people who loved the Lord. They must be men and women who served God not only with their words, but by their actions and in their hearts. It is such a heart that makes God's people cheerful givers, eager workers, joyful singers and sincere worshippers. This is the mark of a true servant of God. Without such a heart we find only the empty ritual described by the prophet:

> These people come near to me with their mouth
> and honour me with their lips,
> but their hearts are far from me.
> Their worship of me
> is made up only of rules taught by men.
> Therefore once more I will astound these people
> with wonder upon wonder;
> the wisdom of the wise will perish,
> the intelligence of the intelligent will vanish
>
> (Isa. 29:13-14).

17.
Ministries in God's house

Please read 1 Chronicles 23:1 - 24:31

Sometimes we displease God because the things we do are wrong in themselves and are never permissible, but at other times we displease him when we do a good thing with a wrong motive. This is rather like the prayers offered by the Pharisees, for although it is good to pray, they prayed in order to be seen and admired by other people. In T. S. Eliot's play, *Murder in the Cathedral* the archbishop, Thomas à Beckett, responds to the third temptation: 'This third is the greatest treason, to do the right thing for the wrong reason.' This is the most subtle and dangerous of all temptations.

David fell into this temptation when he ordered a census of his fighting men (ch. 21). Previously in the history of Israel God had ordered a census of the Israelites (Num. 1), but David ordered this particular census in a spirit of pride and self-reliance and as a result God punished him. In chapter 23 we read of another — very different — census amongst the Israelites. The Levites of thirty years or more were to be counted (23:3) and classified into four groups: those who supervised the work of the temple, officials and judges, gatekeepers, and musicians (23:4-5). Lists of the three later groups are contained in chapters 25-27, while the priests and Levites who supervised the work of the temple are listed in chapters 23-24.

The purpose of this census was God's honour. As David's earthly life drew towards its close he thought increasingly about the work that his son Solomon would take up after he died. Not only would Solomon take over the reigns of power, but he would also build a house for the Lord. David wanted that work to continue without distraction once Solomon started it. He wanted his kingdom to be organized for the purpose of serving God, so that the temple could be constructed with the minimum of confusion. The temple was given great importance in Israel's life because it was the place where God was to be worshipped, and Israel was the one nation on the face of the earth where God was pleased to build his temple. The Levites counted in these chapters were God's servants who ministered in that temple.

Before considering in further detail what we can learn from the priests and Levites, we will note some general considerations which will help us to understand these chapters which record the results of David's second census.

Facts matter in the Bible

Throughout these chapters there is a striking concern for factual detail. Even facts that may not be of much obvious interest or relevance to our generation are recorded; including for instance the fact that Eleazar died without sons (23:22). Like the rest of Chronicles these chapters are the work of a careful historian who investigated a variety of written sources and sought to record the facts of history. He is rather like Luke, the great historian of the New Testament, who set out his purpose in Luke 1:3: 'Therefore, since I myself have carefully investigated everything from the beginning, it seemed good also to me to write an orderly account for you, most excellent

Theophilus, so that you may know the certainty of the things you have been taught.'

The message of the Bible always rests on a solid foundation of facts. Whether it is the Old Testament account of King David, or the New Testament account of Jesus Christ, the facts (or history) come first and then we are given the explanation (or doctrine). If the facts are not accurate, then the explanation has no authority. That linkage between history and doctrine has been questioned by modern views of the authority of Scripture. As Christians we believe that the Bible is inspired (spoken by God as his Word) and infallible (it teaches true doctrine), but we must also insist that the Bible is inerrant (incapable of error). We can take our stand on every fact that is contained in Holy Scripture and insist that it is free from mistakes of any kind. The God of truth can no more mislead us about the history of David's kingdom than he can err in his teaching about the doctrine of justification by faith.

God's people are of great importance to him

These chapters refer to a great many people who are mentioned nowhere else in the whole Bible. Even where they are mentioned again, in many cases only their names are recorded and we know virtually nothing about their lives. They are like many others who lived faithful lives as God's people, but died without history recording their works. But there is no such person as an unnoticed child of God. The Lord's elect are 'sealed with this inscription: "The Lord knows those who are his"' (2 Tim. 2:19). The writer of Hebrews describes God's people as those 'whose names are written in heaven' (Heb. 12:23) and the psalmist tells us that even their tears are counted by God (Ps. 56:8).

These lengthy records of otherwise unknown people who performed routine and often menial tasks in the administration of temple ritual are a powerful reminder of this truth. We who serve Christ as members of 'a holy priesthood, offering spiritual sacrifices acceptable to God through Jesus Christ' (1 Peter 2:5) can also take encouragement from the regard that God has for the labours of his servants.

The past is important for us

Paul taught Timothy that the whole book of Scripture 'is useful for teaching, rebuking, correcting and training in righteousness' (2 Tim. 3:16). This is true not just of the Gospel accounts of our Lord, or the epistles which explain the great doctrines of our faith, or the majestic prophecies of the Old Testament; it is also true of the historical narratives that occupy such a large portion of the canon of Scripture. The Holy Spirit has recorded the experiences of God's people over many years to teach us truths and illustrate principles that we would not otherwise understand with sufficient clarity. Our understanding of God's Word will be greatly impoverished if we ignore the history of God's people in Old Testament times.

J. G. Vos has written a booklet entitled *Ashamed of the Tents of Shem* to describe how many New Testament Christians have forgotten their Jewish heritage from the history of Israel and have even ignored large parts of the Old Testament. This is a great pity because it produces a shallow and imbalanced type of Christianity. It also ignores a large part of the ministry of the Holy Spirit, who worked through men like the Chronicler and other inspired historians to record the lives of God's people in past ages so that we might learn spiritual truth from them (see 1 Cor. 10:1-6). Passages like those we find in these chapters may present us with a challenge, but there is blessing to be enjoyed as we wrestle with their message.

The Levites: organized for God's service (23:6-32; 24:20-31)

Before considering the work done by the Levites we ought to note the numerical growth of the tribe of Levi since the time of Moses. In Numbers 4:47-48 the Levites numbered 8,580 men aged between thirty and fifty, whereas in 1 Chronicles 23:3 there were over 38,000 Levite men aged thirty and over. In percentage terms Levi had grown far more than any of the other tribes. This was God's reward for faithful service, for more than any other tribe the Levites had devoted themselves to the Lord's service. They had no land of their own and were scattered throughout Israel, but the Lord compensated them by making their tribe large and influential.

There are many examples of faithfulness in the history of the tribe of Levi. When the rest of the nation worshipped the golden calf, it was the Levites who stood at Moses' side: 'He stood at the entrance to the camp and said, "Whoever is for the Lord, come to me." And all the Levites rallied to him' (Exod. 32:26). When the rest of the people fell into serious apostasy at Baal Peor it was a member of the tribe of Levi, Phinehas, who purged the evil from the nation's life (Num. 25:7-13). As a result the Lord blessed his tribe and multiplied it. In 23:7-23 we have a representative sample of the tribe of Levi, grouped into the three main clans of chapter 6.

Numbers alone do not always prove to be a blessing. Matthew Henry explains very pithily: 'Number without order is but a clog and an occasion of tumult.' (Anyone who has organized an outing for children will know what that means!) God is a God of order and not confusion, and everything in his church is to be done 'in a fitting and orderly way' (1 Cor. 14:40). In 23:24-32 we are told how the Levites were organized so that they might carry out their ministry in the temple more effectively.

After the building of the temple the Levites had new responsibilities in the light of changed circumstances. Traditionally they had been the carriers of the ark and the tabernacle furnishings while the tabernacle was being moved from place to place through the wilderness and into the promised land. Their service as porters was needed so long as no fixed place of worship had been established, but once the ark was brought to its resting-place in Jerusalem their work was finished. They were in danger of being made redundant!

Redundancy is a word that many people in the modern world have come to dread. A person who has been made redundant has lost more than his employment and income, for he has lost his dignity. He feels like someone who has been dismissed as a superfluous human being — surplus to requirements. However, we may be thankful that in the service of God there is no such thing as a redundant person. All God's people are needed, because when one avenue of service is closed another is opened to them. That is what we see in the ministry of the Levites. When their service as porters was no longer needed, they became responsible for the care of temple, assisting the priests in preparing and offering the sacrifices (23:25-26,32). Their new duties are described in detail in 23:28-31 — maintaining the fabric of the temple, storing and preparing the offerings and praising the Lord in song.

With these new responsibilities the Levites were very busy and additional help was needed. To meet the need the younger Levites between twenty and thirty were brought into active service (see 23:27; cf. Num. 4:35,47; 8:24). In Scripture, while youth and inexperience act as a bar to roles of leadership

(1 Tim. 3:6), they ought not to prove an obstacle or excuse to hinder active service (1 Tim. 4:12).

As well as great changes in the form of ministry undertaken by the Levites, there were also unchanging priorities. The temple, just as much as the tabernacle, was a temporary structure; both would eventually pass away, but God's glory would never pass away. Both the tabernacle and the temple were constructed to reflect God's glory and teach his people how sinners might be reconciled to him. They were places to which God's people would come to return thanks to their Redeemer. Before the temple was built and after Nebuchadnezzar's armies destroyed it in 587 B.C., these were the priorities of the Levites: **'They were to serve before the Lord regularly in the proper number and in the way prescribed for them'** (23:31). In every age God's unchanging priority is to have men and women who will worship him in spirit and truth (John 4:23-24).

The priests: selected for special service (24:1-19)

Out of the tribe of Levi one family was chosen for special service, the family of Aaron (see Exod. 28:1; Num. 17; Ps. 105:26; 106:16). After lowly service as Moses' spokesman, Aaron and his family became the priests who served the Lord at the very centre of Israel's life, while Moses' sons merely became ordinary Levites (23:13-14). This was according to God's sovereign choice, for he raises up one and brings down another in his wisdom and good pleasure (see Isa. 64:8; Jer. 18:6; Rom. 9:21).

Although David organized the priests for their service at the altar (24:3), the hand of God can be clearly seen in the distribution of responsibilities among the priests. The priests were divided into twenty-four **'divisions'**, or 'courses', to take their turn in ministering at the altar. This system continued until New Testament times when we read of Zechariah, a member of the priestly division of Abijah, ministering at the altar in the days of Herod, King of Judah (compare 24:10 with Luke 1:5).

The order in which these priestly divisions came to minister at the altar was determined by drawing lots (24:5). Drawing lots was a method of discovering God's will in important matters when there was no existing guidance, or at least not sufficiently precise guidance. This method was used to select the animal which would be the scapegoat on the Day of Atonement (Lev. 16:10), to allocate the promised land among the tribes (Josh. 18-19) and to select Matthias as an apostle to replace Judas (Acts 1:26). After prayer and heart preparation the lot was cast and its decision revealed God's will, for according to Proverbs 16:33, 'The lot is cast into the lap, but its every decision is from the Lord.'

It is sometimes asked whether the casting of lots remains an appropriate way for Christians to discern the Lord's will today. The answer is probably not, because of two important developments since the last use of lots that is recorded with God's approval in Scripture. First of all, we now have a completed book of Scripture that gives a full and final revelation of all that God wishes us to know about salvation and Christian living on earth. Then, secondly, the regenerate person has the mind of Christ as a guide given in fulness since the ministry of the Holy Spirit at Pentecost (1 Cor. 2:15-16). When the New Testament church after Pentecost sent out missionaries or selected elders there is no record of their using lots, but we do read of fervent prayer and the thoughtful consideration of biblical qualifications.

Returning to David and the organization of the Old Testament priests into divisions by use of lots, let us consider some lessons we might learn from this process.

1. The priesthood was selected by God and not by man

A priest, after all, is to stand as a mediator reconciling a holy
God and sinful men. The priestly office was not open to just
any man, and certainly not to a man who appointed himself.
The writer of Hebrews explains the theology that underlay the
Old Testament priesthood: 'Every high priest is selected from
among men and is appointed to represent them in matters
related to God... No one takes this honour upon himself; he
must be called by God, just as Aaron was' (Heb. 5:1,4). Even
when God's Son came as the 'one mediator between God and
men', he did not take the priesthood upon himself, but was
appointed to it by his Father (Heb. 5:5-6). No man can appoint
his own way of salvation, nor can any present himself as an
acceptable mediator. There is only one way of salvation, and
that way was opened by the priesthood of God's appointment.

2. The priestly ministry was never-ending

Some emergency services are so essential that even at week-
ends or during holidays there is a doctor or chemist available
on a rota basis. In the temple in Jerusalem the priests were so
organized that there was always a division on duty to offer
sacrifices on behalf of the people. **'They were ... to stand
every morning to thank and praise the Lord. They were to
do the same in the evening and whenever burnt offerings
were presented to the Lord on Sabbaths and at New Moon
festivals and at appointed feasts'** (23:30-31). Although
these verses refer directly to the ordinary Levites, they show
that the priests too were constantly offering sacrifices. Even
when there was bereavement in the high priest's family no
compassionate leave was allowed because of the importance
of their ministry on the people's behalf (see Lev. 10:6-7).

Consequently there were twenty-four divisions allocated their place by lot so that the offerings might be made without interruption for want of consecrated priests.

During the siege of Leningrad during the Second World War the priests of the Russian Orthodox Church ensured that the divine liturgy was being said round the clock in at least one of the city's churches. The prayer vigil for their city was as constant as the ministry of the Old Testament. Yet the ministry of the temple priests is not so much a challenge to us to 'Pray without ceasing' as a pointer to the priestly ministry of our Saviour who is the true and everlasting propitiation for our sins.

It is the Lord Jesus who stands between sinners and an angry God to take away sins. It is important to distinguish between his act of atonement (making a payment once for all time for the sins of his people, paying their debt, destroying the power of sin and effecting reconciliation with God) and his ministry of intercession. The first is an action never to be repeated, extended or re-enacted (Heb. 7:27; 9:26-28), whereas the second is an ongoing ministry in heaven from the moment of his ascension until the end of this age (Heb. 7:24-25). Without Christ's finished priesthood we have no foundation on which to base our salvation, but without his ongoing intercession we have no application of redemption or the experience of sins forgiven.

It is possible to go to the chemist's shop only to find that its doors are closed, or to a doctor's surgery only to discover that the doctor is not available. There is never a moment (until the day of Christ's return) when a sinner can flee to Christ for salvation and find that there is no Saviour to hear him. Until the Day of Judgement we live in a day of grace during which Christ prays for his elect so that they will most certainly come to him for forgiveness. During this day of grace there is never a moment when the believer is exposed to the wrath of God without the blood of Christ to cover him. There is never a moment when the child of God is not covered by the prayers of his Lord and Saviour just as a chick is covered by its mother's wings. What a blessing that his priesthood is a continual ministry of intercession for his people!

18.
Serving the Lord in many ways

Please read 1 Chronicles 25:1 - 27:34

L. S. Lowry is one of England's best-known painters of modern times. His paintings have a unique and unmistakable style, set against the mills and factories and terraced houses of northern England. The scenes they depict are crowded with people: men coming from or going to their work, women doing their shopping, children playing, vagrants wandering — all painted very simply as matchstick people. In this way a whole community going about its business is depicted. The section of 1 Chronicles we have now reached is like a verbal portrait of the people of Israel in the style of L. S. Lowry. We have a view of a great many ordinary Israelites, but their everyday lives are depicted against the backdrop of the temple in Jerusalem rather than a factory or blast furnace.

From chapter 10 onwards the Chronicler has been following the sequence of David's reign, beginning with the death of Saul and continuing until David's ill-fated census of his fighting men. Chapters 23-27 are a break from that sequence in which the Chronicler looks ahead to the time when the temple was completed and its ministry had commenced and he describes the Levites, priests and other servants who served in the temple. Before his death David appointed these men to their work so that when Solomon acceded to the throne he could devote his energy to building the temple.

David was given a unique authority and the gift of administration so that the system he established lasted for many
centuries after his death, and was re-established when the Jews
returned to Judea after the exile in Babylon. When the returning exiles sought to organize the temple worship in a proper
and God-honouring way they looked back to David as their
model, and the Chronicler's history became their textbook.

As Christians living in an age when there is no longer any
need for an earthly temple and earthly sacrifices, we do not
seek to re-establish the pattern set by David's reforms, but
there are lessons in Christian service that we can learn from the
many ways in which these men served the Lord. In these
chapters there are five groups of people whose work we shall
consider: the singers (25:1-31), the gatekeepers (26:1-19), the
officials (26:20-32), the army officers (27:1-24) and the overseers of the king's property (27:25-34).

The singers honoured God by leading the praise (25:1-31)

These were Levites set aside by David to take charge of the
temple music and lead the people in praising God. Their contribution to God's worship is described as **'the ministry of
prophesying, accompanied by harps, lyres and cymbals'**
(25:1), with the reference to prophecy being twice repeated
(25:2,3). The words used in the praise of God are very important and they were to be prophetic words, or words that spoke
of God. This does not mean that the singers composed songs
spontaneously when they praised God, but that they used
words of praise that had been given to them by God's prophets
so that the greatness of the Lord might be declared in song.

David was a man through whom God's Spirit spoke, and
many years later Peter the apostle recognized him as a prophet
(see 2 Sam. 23:2; Acts 2:30). Under David's leadership there

was an important prophetic movement in Israel through which God revealed great truths about himself and his salvation. Men like Asaph and Heman wrote songs which reveal a deep and sensitive knowledge of God, and we are told that these men **'were under the supervision of the king'** (25:6). So too were the men who sang the songs of praise that David and other inspired songwriters had composed (25:2). As a result the praise they offered to God was pure and edifying for God's people. The words that are sung in worship have a great influence on the spiritual life of the church for, as R. J. George of Pittsburgh has asserted, 'It is difficult to corrupt the doctrines of a church where it holds to scriptural worship.' The reason why the singers were so important was that they prophesied the great truths of Scripture in Israel's praise.

The singers are listed according to their families in 25:2-5 and in verses 6-7 we gain an insight into how these Levitical families trained their young people to maintain the true worship of God. Sons were trained under the supervision of their fathers (25:2,3,6) so that they became skilful in the service they performed (25:7). To do anything well requires dedicated effort, and the praise of God is no exception. If we are to praise God from the heart we must study to understand the words we sing, meditating on their rich spiritual meaning; and if we are to commend God by the way we praise him, congregations of his people must spare no effort to ensure that their praise is as tuneful and as excellent as possible. Otherwise God's worship is treated with contempt.

The Chronicler notes the responsibilities of fathers in this regard, for it was fathers who trained their sons to sing. Too often Christian training in the home is left to mothers, but that is not the lesson taught by the example of these Levitical families.

Like the priests who ministered at the altar, the Levite singers were divided into twenty-four divisions which were allocated their places in a rota (25:8-31). This division of responsibility allowed for a continual response of thanksgiving from God's people for his blood-bought mercy. Ongoing praise is the only appropriate response to the everlasting salvation purchased by Jesus Christ: 'Through Jesus, therefore, let us continually offer to God a sacrifice of praise — the fruit of lips that confess his name' (Heb. 13:15).

The gatekeepers honoured God by humble service (26:1-19)

The service of these gatekeepers was not so public as that of the singers. The list of gatekeepers given here in 26:1-11 most probably refers to those who were allocated responsibilities in the time of King David, whereas the list already given in 9:17-21 refers to those from the families of the gatekeepers who returned from the exile. The account in chapter 9 is of interest in our study of this passage because it describes the work the gatekeepers did. In that chapter we are told that they 'were entrusted with the responsibility for the rooms and treasuries in the house of God' (9:26). More specifically, 'They would spend the night stationed round the house of God, because they had to guard it; and they had charge of the key for opening it each morning' (9:27).

Their work was a humble work and required a lowly spirit. That spirit is reflected in Psalm 84:10: 'I would rather be a doorkeeper in the house of my God than dwell in the tents of the wicked.' It cannot have been easy to stand outside in the heat of the sun while the focus of everyone's attention was inside with the praise and the sacrifices. Yet in this chapter the importance of their work is recognized.

The significance of the gatekeepers' work lay not so much in what they *did* as in what they *prevented*. Their job was to keep the temple free from unwelcome visitors or anything that would defile the building so as to hinder the important ministry that was conducted within its precincts. In 22:19 David described the temple as a 'sanctuary', or holy place. This does not mean that any location is physically nearer to heaven than others, or that God automatically manifests his blessing in certain places. Crude ideas like that can be dismissed immediately; but certain locations are holy because of what takes place at them, such as the burning bush where God spoke to Moses in Exodus 3:5.

This was the case with the temple, because God had appointed it as the place where sacrifices were to be offered to him; and within the temple the Holy of Holies was a room into which only the high priest might enter, and that only once a year. A partition was to be erected around the temple precincts lest the entrance of any defilement should spoil what was holy within it. Nehemiah 13:4-9 describes how that happened while Eliashib was priest after the return from exile. Eliashib was friendly with Tobiah, the Ammonite ruler, and had allowed him to use the temple to store his personal belongings. When Nehemiah found out what had been happening he was incensed and ordered that the temple precincts be purified, for this was not how a holy place ought to be used. It was abuses of the temple such as this that the gatekeepers had been appointed to prevent.

The importance of the gatekeepers' work is shown not just by what happened in the days of Nehemiah, when their work had fallen into abeyance, but by the care taken by David to ensure that all the gates were continually guarded by these men (see 26:12-19). There were four approaches to the temple and four gates; and lots were cast to allocate gatekeepers to their station (26:13). Teams of gatekeepers were allocated to each gate so that a constant watch might be kept over each entrance — four Levites a day on each to the northern and southern gates, with a further two at the storehouse, four on the approach to the western court and two at the court itself. The eastern gate was the busiest as it led to the main entrance to the temple, so it was guarded by a team of six Levites each day (see 26:17-18).

The work of the gatekeepers is like the lives of many godly people which are never exposed to the public view. Often their importance is recognized only when their work has not been done. Frequently their quiet faithfulness, their steadfast prayerfulness, or the witness that such a believer bears in a trying situation is appreciated only when that person has passed from this life. Then when he or she is no longer able to carry on the work Satan has a freer hand as a result. We should never consider it a trivial thing to keep a door in the house of God, if we can thereby maintain the purity and beauty of his church.

The officials honoured God by their stewardship of his possessions (26:20-32)

Part of the gatekeepers' responsibility was to watch over the treasuries of God's house and these officials were a specialist group dedicated to this work. They were given charge over the temple finances, which appear to have been divided into a general fund (26:22) and funds dedicated by named individuals to specific purposes (26:20,26-28).

As well as the diaconal responsibility for material resources, attention was given to the human resources of the nation (26:30-32). These verses show a concern for the portion of the nation that did not live within easy reach of Jerusalem, especially the tribes living on the east side of the River Jordan — the Reubenites, the Gadites and the half-tribe of Manasseh.

The danger was that these isolated tribes might be lost to the true religion of Israel because it was much harder for them to come up to the temple in Jerusalem to worship and they were more subject to heathen influence.

David ordered that the records of all Israel be kept as complete as possible so that no section of Israel might be lost because of bureaucratic error. The danger of being overlooked by impersonal bureaucrats is not something peculiar to our modern age! To ensure that no part of his nation was forgotten about, David put able men like Jeriah and his family in charge of the Transjordanian tribes **'for every matter pertaining to God and for the affairs of the king'** (26:32). David's concern was both for their physical welfare as citizens of Israel and for their spiritual welfare as members of the covenant people.

Scripture teaches us to have a similar concern for the spiritual welfare of others, especially those who have drifted in their faith: 'Brothers, if someone is caught in a sin, you who are spiritual should restore him gently' (Gal. 6:1). 'If one of you should wander from the truth and someone should bring him back, remember this: whoever turns a sinner from the error of his way will save him from death and cover over a multitude of sins' (James 5:19-20).

The officers honoured God by protecting the king (27:1-24)

The whole nation, and not just the Levites, were involved in protecting the king. Twelve divisions of 24,000 men were appointed to serve as a royal bodyguard for one month in the year, the commanding officer of each division being mentioned by name in 27:2-15. Other officers are mentioned in 27:16-22. This protection was of great importance because the king was the Lord's anointed and was entitled to the nation's loyalty. For this reason David refused to kill Saul while he was king. Yet anyone in a position of authority becomes a target for attack, and David's status made him an obvious target for satanic attack. Satan would have been very glad to undermine King David because an attack on the Lord's anointed is always an attack on God himself.

Although Christians do not take up worldly weapons to defend the honour of the Lord Jesus, they are involved in a spiritual warfare. We are urged to put on the breastplate of righteousness and the helmet of salvation and to take up the shield of faith and the sword of the Spirit which is the Word of God. The purpose of our warfare is to defend the honour of our Saviour, defeat his enemies and extend his kingdom. In this we ought to be zealous in guarding the honour of King Jesus, just as the royal bodyguard sought to protect David. John Bunyan, in his allegorical tale *The Pilgrim's Progress,* created the figure Mr Valiant-for-the-truth, who ought to be an inspiration to us all.

We also need to be zealous to protect ourselves from temptation, because the times when greatest dishonour is done to Christ are when those who profess to love him fall into sin. 'Be on your guard; stand firm in the faith; be men of courage; be strong. Do everything in love' (1 Cor. 16:13-14). Our constant prayer ought to be: 'Set a guard over my mouth, O Lord; keep watch over the door of my lips' (Ps. 141:3).

The overseers honoured God in their secular employment (27:25-34)

The final list of David's servants refers to men whose work had no obvious reference to the temple, or to the spiritual life of the nation. As we read these verses we are struck by how ordinary their tasks sound. There is work that we may have done ourselves: management of crops, or keeping livestock, providing food for the household; the list includes those who gave advice and leaders in the army. Yet each of these men was doing kingdom work because he was serving the king.

Sometimes we talk of people entering full-time service for the Lord. What we should say is that a person is going to serve the Lord as a pastor or as a missionary, because every Christian is (or ought to be) in full-time service for the Lord, whatever the area of his or her service. For some the field of the service may be in areas that we often call 'secular', as were those mentioned in these verses (farming the land, or supplying olive oil); while others may 'labour in the word and doctrine' (1 Tim. 5:17, NKJV). In either case the labour is unto the Lord our King.

Conclusion

As we look back over the five types of service rendered by the men described in these chapters there are two common features that ought to be noted.

1. They were consecrated men

A frequent refrain is the theme that their service was for the king (see 25:2,6; 26:32; 27:1). At the centre of everything was the towering figure of King David. He was the moving force in organizing his people, and loyalty to him was what motivated their service. The New Testament teaches that loyalty to Christ is not displayed in religious exercises only, but in everything we do. 'Whether you eat or drink or whatever you do, do it all for the glory of God' (1 Cor. 10:31).

2. *They were useful men*

Two other frequently used words to describe the men in these chapters are 'skilled' and 'able' (the Hebrew word means 'mighty'). These men were useful because they were competent to do things for the Lord and because they were energetic in doing them. But the main reason for their usefulness was that both their ability and their energy were consecrated to the king for the service of God.

Great gifts that are not consecrated to the Lord can become a problem. Absalom was a young man with great ability, but he was not a consecrated man and his strengths led the kingdom into a destructive civil war. We can only speculate about the good he might have done had his gifts been consecrated to the Lord. Robert Murray M'Cheyne once wrote in a letter to a friend that it is not great giftedness that God uses so much as great likeness to Christ. These chapters show us the enormous potential of a large number of ordinary people whose humble gifts are consecrated to God.

19.
Chosen to be a servant

Please read 1 Chronicles 28:1-21

One of the most honourable titles in the Scriptures is that of a 'servant'. In the clearest Old Testament descriptions of the work of our Saviour, Isaiah described him as a servant (Isa. 42:1; 49:3,6; 52:13; 53:11). Our Lord himself said during his earthly life, 'I am among you as one who serves' (Luke 22:27) and demonstrated his willingness to serve by washing his disciples' feet. Since their Master acted as a servant, so too did his disciples; both James and Peter introduced themselves in their letters as 'a servant ... of Jesus Christ' (James 1:1; 2 Peter 1:1).

The final two chapters of 1 Chronicles are set against the background of a grand state occasion. As David grew older and felt his strength declining he wanted to establish Solomon as the heir to his throne. He gathered together **'the officers over the tribes, the commanders of the divisions ... and the officials in charge of all the property and livestock ... together with the palace officials, the mighty men and all the brave warriors'** (28:1) and he presented Solomon to them as their new king. In chapter 29 we shall find David's words to them acknowledging Solomon as his heir. Meanwhile, in chapter 28, David gave some words of counsel to his son. Lest Solomon should be carried away with the importance of his new position and the fact that he was the centre of the nation's attention, David reminded him that he was a servant — of God and of his people.

Solomon was chosen by God to serve (28:2-10)

David never tired of telling what God had done for him and in these verses he recounts how God had blocked his own ambition to build a temple for the Lord, but had promised that his son Solomon would build the temple for him. Throughout the narrative the emphasis falls upon God's sovereign decision. David told the people, **'I had it in my heart...'**, but his desires did not come to fruition: **'But God said to me, "You are not to build a house"'** (28:2,3). Man may propose, but it is God who disposes, and at every stage it was God's choice that decided what would happen.

The sovereignty of God is taught in these verses by referring to a series of strategic choices that God had made. It was God who chose the tribe of Judah to produce the royal line, and David's family to be the royal family (28:4). Out of David's large family God chose one of his sons to succeed him and to build the house of God. God does not always pick the most obvious candidates. As we have already seen in our study of the tribe of Judah in chapter 2, Judah had not always been a paragon of virtue or a good example to the other tribes (see Gen. 38) but in spite of their blemishes they were the chosen tribe. In spite of the fact that David was the youngest and least experienced son from an obscure Bethlehemite family, he was selected to succeed Saul as king. Then in choosing Solomon God did not take the oldest or the most natural choice. We should not allow Solomon's later achievements to blind us to his youthful inexperience at this time (28:5-7; cf. 1 Kings 3:7). Yet God chose him.

God is not swayed by the factors that influence our decisions, for he is sovereign in choosing who will serve him. An obvious example of that sovereign freedom is our Lord's choice of disciples, who were taken from their worldly occupations to follow him. In John 15:16 Jesus told them, 'You did not choose me, but I choose you and appointed you to go and bear fruit.' This is true not only of those who serve God in a public capacity, for in Romans 16 there is a list of ordinary members of the church in Rome, one of whom was 'Rufus, chosen in the Lord' (Rom. 16:13). Those who love the Lord as their Saviour do so only because God has chosen them and opened their hearts to accept his gospel: 'All who were appointed for eternal life believed' (Acts 13:48); 'So then it is not of him who wills, nor of him who runs, but of God who shows mercy' (Rom. 9:16, NKJV); 'For he chose us in him before the creation of the world' (Eph. 1:4). This is a solemn and searching truth, and in these verses David sought to apply it to Solomon's life.

In 28:8-9 David charged Solomon with the *responsibilities* that his exalted position would bring. W. S. Gilbert wrote of the members of the British aristocracy who sat in the House of Lords that 'They did nothing in particular and did it very well.' Their privileges did not seem to carry especially onerous responsibilities, but for Solomon it would be very different. He would achieve something that David had only dreamed about, for he would see the glory of God descend into the finished temple. Solomon would inherit the blessings of peaceful possession of Israel, **'this good land'** for which his father had had to struggle. With these blessings came many responsibilities. Solomon would be obliged to care for the kingdom that he had inherited so that it might be passed on to succeeding generations, for he held his blessings in trust and would be required to give an account of his service.

Moreover Solomon could never take God's favour for granted. The fact that God had chosen him as his beloved servant meant that he owed a very great debt of love to God. In verse 9 we find the words and phrases that the Chronicler commonly used to describe the true piety of those who love the Lord. Solomon was not to sit back and wait for God's blessing, but was to **'serve him with wholehearted devotion and with a willing mind'**. The promise came with a warning: **'If you seek him, he will be found by you; but if you forsake him, he will reject you for ever'** (28:9).

It is only a serious misunderstanding of the doctrine of God's sovereignty that allows it to become an excuse for carelessness in the lives of his people. As well as emphasizing the sovereignty of God's choice in selecting his people, the Scriptures frequently highlight God's purpose in election. In John 15:16 our Lord told his disciples that they had been chosen 'to go and bear fruit'. Similarly when Paul taught the Ephesian believers that their election and salvation were not built upon their good works, he reminded them that their election was unto good works: 'For we are God's workmanship, created in Christ Jesus to do good works, which God prepared in advance for us to do' (Eph. 2:10; cf. Titus 2:14).

The final application of the truth of God's sovereignty in choosing Solomon for the task that lay ahead of him was one that afforded David *reassurance* of God's support. Solomon could enter his life's work secure in the knowledge that it was not overweening ambition that had brought him to the throne, but the will of God. He could count on the Lord, who had chosen him and called him to build the temple, to continue with him as his helper and guide. David urged him to think long and hard about the implications of that fact: **'Consider now, for the Lord has chosen you.'** The challenge for Solomon was to **'Be strong and to do the work'** (28:10). He was to be strong in faith and in confidence and in zeal as he did the work to which God had called him. What more can any child of God ask for?

Solomon would be directed by God in the service he gave (28:11-19)

On the face of it these verses might seem like David's attempt to control Solomon from the grave, as he left detailed instructions for the construction of the temple and its furnishings. A great deal of resentment can be caused when a retiring leader finds it difficult to allow his successor to get on with his work. Constant unsought interference can very quickly cause friction. Yet that is not what the Chronicler describes in these verses.

David left detailed plans for the temple and its interior (28:11) and the division of duties amongst the priests and Levites, already described in chapters 23-26 (28:13). Then the weight of gold to be used in making the various items of temple furniture was set out in some detail (28:14-18). David was very careful not to present this as interference in the work that God had given to Solomon. God had spoken through David (who was after all a prophet) to show Solomon how to approach the work that lay before him, for **'The Spirit had put [the plans] in his mind'** (28:12). Just as on Mount Sinai God had given Moses the plans according to which Bezalel and others constructed the tabernacle, so now David was God's mouthpiece with instructions for the son who would follow him. **'"All this," David said, "I have in writing from the hand of the Lord upon me, and he gave me understanding in all the details of the plan"'** (28:19).

In this way Solomon would learn a submissive spirit, as he took heed of God's instructions given through his father. Later he would write the book of Proverbs as a book of instruction for his own son:

> Listen, my son, to your father's instruction
>   and do not forsake your mother's teaching.
> They will be a garland to grace your head
>   and a chain to adorn your neck
>
> (Prov. 1:8-9).

Before giving advice like that Solomon had to learn to take it, because only the person who can submit to authority will have any credibility when he seeks to exercise it.

Moreover Solomon learned to submit to God's direction. David had needed to learn this lesson when he accepted that Solomon would build the temple (28:2-3). Whatever plans Solomon might have had for the construction and furnishing of the temple had to be laid aside in favour of God's clearly revealed will in these verses. Throughout Solomon's life, and in many other areas of endeavour, there would have to be changes and corrections when his plans were out of line with God's. There might be disappointment, and even frustration, but God's plans must always have the priority since we are God's servants and he is the supervisor of our work. These verses are the detailed instructions of the Supervisor.

It should come as no surprise that God gave so many precise instructions to Solomon for the building of the temple. It was, after all, going to be the Lord's house, and he wanted every part of it to be perfect. As we consider the detail contained in these written instructions we are reminded of the completeness of God's sovereignty over our lives. Abraham Kuyper encouraged Christians to consider the serious implications of this truth when he wrote that 'There is no area of our lives about which Jesus Christ does not say, "It is mine."' It is not sufficient that we recognize God's authority in the grand, public gestures; he must govern the very details of our daily living — how we earn our living, how we spend our time and our money, how we choose our friends, the books we read, the programmes we watch on television. These and many other details must be arranged in accordance with God's revealed will for us.

Solomon was strengthened by God (28:20-21)

One of the frailties of fallen human nature is that we do not always take advice easily, especially if it takes the form of detailed instructions. Yet David's purpose was not to frustrate Solomon with unsought advice, but to encourage him and his people as they faced the many challenges that lay ahead. It is on that note that he brings this chapter to a conclusion: **'Be strong and courageous, and do the work'** (28:20). David focused Solomon's attention on two blessings.

1. The Lord was with him

'Do not be afraid or discouraged, for the Lord God, my God, is with you' (28:20). It was a comfort to know that David's God would be with Solomon. The God who had led David into battle and had never deserted him, the God who had chastised David when he sinned but restored him when he repented, the God who had confirmed his covenant with David — that is the Lord who would be with Solomon. The promise that had been made to David was extended to Solomon as well: 'If you seek him, he will be found by you' (28:9).

It is of great importance for God's people that they make every effort to know God's will for their lives, for there is no safer place for us than the one where God wants us to be. It was in the place of God's choice for them that both David and Solomon knew God's blessing in such rich measure. God's will for us may not be what we would have chosen for ourselves, and it might not be what appears attractive or

pleasant, but it is always what is best for us. God may call us
to serve him in a situation of testing, but he will always be with
us while we are there, and that is blessing enough. When Paul
found himself in Corinth during his second missionary journey he went through a deep trough of despair. After many
discouragements in that pagan city the Lord spoke to reassure
Paul: 'Do not be afraid; keep on speaking, do not be silent. For
I am with you...' (Acts 18:9). The Lord Jesus repeated his
Great Commission when he appeared to Paul that night in a
dream. He not only renewed Paul's calling to preach the
gospel, but reassured him of his strengthening presence: 'And
surely I am with you always, to the very end of the age' (Matt.
28:20). There is no greater blessing for which anyone can ask.

2. *The Lord's people were with him*

**'The divisions of the priests and Levites are ready for all
the work on the temple of God, and every willing man
skilled in any craft will help you in all the work. The
officials and all the people will obey your every command'**
(28:21). This verse summarizes the significance of all the lists
in chapters 23-27. All the Israelites mentioned there had been
willing supporters of David and would support Solomon in the
work that lay ahead. During the Second World War the British
government produced a poster to encourage the whole nation
to support the war effort. It depicted the beaming face of Sir
Winston Churchill and the slogan: 'Let us go forward together.' One man on his own could not win the war, but the
nation united behind its leader could.

If the temple was to be built and the kingdom extended, the
whole nation must be united around the Lord's anointed —
Solomon, David's son. Solomon could not do the work on his
own but would rely, perhaps more than he realized, on the
willing support of his people. The history of the church shows

that when God does a great work amongst his people he frequently brings together very special combinations of his people. The great preachers and theologians are important, but so too are their lieutenants and the many others who pray for them. Luther could not have achieved what he did without a Melanchthon beside him and a Katherine von Bora at home. Nor could the preaching of a Spurgeon have won so many for Christ without the faithful deacons who worked with him and the many more who prayed for him.

When God saves his people he brings them into the family of a local church, and each believer is placed there to encourage the others. We need to know that we are not alone in serving God in this sinful world. We need to know that there are others who love the Lord and share a delight in the precious truths of God's grace. We need to know that God's people are with us. That was a great encouragement for Solomon, and we ought to seek it for ourselves.

20.
A generous God and a willing people

Please read 1 Chronicles 29:1-30

The summer of 1843 was a momentous one in the spiritual life of Scotland. In May of that year almost 500 ministers left the General Assembly of the Church of Scotland because of the terrible abuse of patronage in the Established Church. Believing that patronage was an invasion of the kingly authority of Jesus Christ within his own church, these men left to form the 'Church of Scotland, Free'. Many of them left their meeting-houses and their manses and, together with their congregations, they worshipped in the open air. As these new congregations built places of worship the members of the Established Church mocked, 'The Free Kirk is the wee kirk, the kirk without the steeple,' to which the reply came: 'The Auld Kirk is the cauld kirk, the kirk without the people.' What indeed is the value of owning impressive buildings if there are not the people willing to worship in them?

This was the question that weighed upon King David as he prepared to hand over his kingdom to Solomon his son. David had planned to build a magnificent temple in Jerusalem for the Lord, but had been prevented from doing so. Solomon was the man God wanted to complete this work, but David devoted his remaining days to preparations for Solomon's building project. Part of David's preparatory work was to leave behind him a willing people who would support Solomon and worship

God in the temple to be built. David instructed his people in the knowledge of God and trained them to be eager in the Lord's service. In this final chapter we gain an insight into this valuable legacy.

As in chapter 28, the scene is set in a gathering of the leaders of all Israel who had been assembled to acknowledge Solomon as David's successor. It was not uncommon for a king to stage his successor's coronation before his own death to ensure a smooth transition from one king to the next. This would appear to be the case at the end of David's reign, and at this national assembly a kind of co-regency was established in Israel. In chapter 28 David addressed words of counsel to Solomon, but in chapter 29 he turned his attention to the people of Israel. They are addressed in these verses.

David's personal generosity (29:1-9)

These verses describe the generous provision that David made for Solomon in the years to come. He had noted both Solomon's weaknesses and the magnitude of the task that awaited him. At the outset he told the assembled gathering that **'The task is great, because this palatial structure is not for man but for the Lord God'** (29:1). The task of building a temple to display the richness of God's mercy to sinners would daunt anyone with even an elementary understanding of God's greatness and mercy, and as David studied the plans revealed by the Lord in 28:19 his amazement could only have grown. So too did his willingness to give to the work.

There follows an impressive list of the valuable items given by David: gold, silver, bronze, iron and wood, onyx, marble and other valuable stones — **'all of these in large quantities'** (29:2). Some features of David's generosity call for special comment.

1. He gave exhaustively

'With all my resources I have provided for the temple of my God' (29:2). It is possible for wealthy people to give large amounts to the Lord's work, but not to give generously because they hold back far more than they give. Jesus saw an example of that as he sat at the temple treasury and watched 'many rich people' throwing in large amounts. He was more impressed by the generosity of a poor widow who gave her two copper coins, 'worth only a fraction of a penny', because 'She, out of her poverty, put in everything' (Mark 12:41-44). David differed from this poor widow only in that he had far more to give, but with all his resources he gave to the Lord's work.

It is hard to give a cut and dried answer when people ask, 'How much ought I to give to the Lord?' The basic offering of God's people is the tithe, or one tenth of their income (Mal. 3:8-10; Matt. 23:23), but the tithe is not a gift to God; it is simply returning to God what is his. We ought to regard it as the platform on which our giving is built rather than a ceiling which indicates a maximum level of giving, for only after we have returned our tithe does our giving become a free-will offering. There will then be times of special need in the life of the church which call for sacrificial giving. Then the only bounds set to our giving to the Lord's work will be the limits of our wealth and our lawful obligations to others. How different is David's example from the unworthy example of Ananias and Sapphira, who made a public show of generosity to the Lord's work by selling their property to give it to the church, but secretly kept back part of the proceeds for themselves! (Acts 5:2).

2. He gave personally

'Besides, in my devotion to the temple of my God I now give my personal treasures' (29:3). The gifts referred to in 29:2

did not come from the public purse, or from the spoils of war, which might not have been considered much of a sacrifice to David. Consider how easily modern politicians promise to spend taxpayers' money! David did not make easy promises like that, for he is the man who said earlier, 'I will not ... sacrifice a burnt offering that costs me nothing' (21:24). These gifts came directly from David's personal wealth. There is the element of sacrifice that is the essence of true generosity.

3. He gave in an exemplary fashion

Not only David, but some of the leading families of the nation **'gave willingly'** (29:6). Their gifts are listed in verses 7-8 and the Chronicler goes on to describe how the effect of David's generosity rippled out to influence many more: **'The people rejoiced at the willing response of their leaders, for they had given freely and wholeheartedly to the Lord'** (29:9). David watched on as this infectious generosity spread: **'David the king also rejoiced greatly.'**

We should not imagine that David's giving to the Lord's work was showy or ostentatious. God has no love for such giving and does not add his blessing to it (Matt. 6:1-4). But generosity such as David had shown could not have been hidden. The very movement of the funds mentioned in these verses would have attracted attention. Moreover, David challenged his people to focus their attention, not upon himself as an example, but upon the Lord as their Sovereign to be honoured: **'Now, who is willing to consecrate himself today to the Lord?'** (29:5).

David recognized God's honour (29:10-20)

We might wonder why the Chronicler was so concerned to record the material gifts given by David and his subjects for the building of the Lord's temple. Sometimes people are suspicious of church leaders who lay great stress on the Christian's duty to give to the Lord's work. Perhaps they think of disreputable characters like some modern tele-evangelists, or of men in a previous age like Tetzel, whose attempts to raise money for the building of St Peter's Basilica in Rome provoked Martin Luther to such indignation.

It is true that God's first concern is with our souls rather than our money, but our stewardship of money is a reflection of what our hearts are like. It was because David's heart was right with God that he was willing to give as generously as he did. The Chronicler then gives us an insight into David's relationship with God. One of the features of the Chronicler's history is his emphasis on prayer, for he frequently quotes lengthy excerpts from the prayers of the people about whom he writes. These prayers are often comments on God's dealings with Israel and on the spiritual condition of the people. In these verses we find the prayer that David prayed in the presence of his people and there are three emphases in it that call for special comment.

1. David praised God for who he is (29:10-13)

David was never ashamed to show the depth of his devotion to God. As a younger man he had danced and rejoiced before the ark of the Lord (15:29); now as an older man he showed the same delight, only in a less energetic way. Before a large gathering of his subjects David prayed with great reverence:

> **Praise be to you, O Lord,**
> **God of our father Israel,**
> **from everlasting to everlasting**
>
> (29:10).

David was not afraid to admit to his subjects that he himself was subject to a higher King. As the emotional intensity of his prayer rose David continued:

> **Yours, O Lord, is the greatness and the power,**
>   **and the glory and the majesty and the splendour,**
>   **for everything in heaven and earth is yours.**
> **Yours, O Lord, is the kingdom;**
>   **you are exalted as head over all**
>
>   **(29:11).**

It is a testimony to the importance of such praise in the prayers of God's people that several phrases from these verses have become familiar to us through the Lord's prayer, which is our model in prayer. Its conclusion, 'For yours is the kingdom and the power and the glory for ever,' summarizes David's words of praise (Matt. 6:13; cf. Rev. 4:11; 5:13). Because wealth and honour come from God, David freely admits that all he has given is simply a thanksgiving to God for all that he has given him:

> **Now, our God, we give you thanks,**
>   **and praise your glorious name**
>
>   **(29:13).**

There is no room in this prayer for the pride of the self-made man!

2. David looked at himself and saw himself for what he was (29:14-17)

David recognized that neither he nor his people deserved the privileges they enjoyed (29:14-15). It was only because of

God's goodness that they were any different from the heathen nations all around them who were still **'aliens and strangers'** in God's eyes. God had taken the people of Israel out of spiritual darkness and entered into a covenant of life with them so that they might call him their Father. It was through the grace of God that they could contemplate building the temple, and it was because of God's generous provision that they had the resources to commence the work. **'As for all this abundance that we have provided for building you a temple for your Holy Name, it comes from your hand, and all of it belongs to you'** (29:16).

The realization that everything we have is a gift from God challenges every temptation to pride. David saw that God's generosity, as well as being a blessing, was a test of his people's hearts. God was like the master in the parable who gave talents to his servants and then called them to give an account of their service (Luke 19:11-26). What does God expect from his people? First of all, he expects us to acknowledge that everything we possess is from him. Then, secondly, he expects us to respond to his goodness with gratitude and generosity. This is what David did, both in his prayers and by his generous giving to the Lord's work.

3. David prayed for wholehearted generosity amongst his people (29:18-20)

From verse 18 onwards the thrust of David's prayer changes from acknowledgement to petition. David prayed for his people and for his son Solomon that they would continue in this spirit of generosity. The habits of giving to the Lord which David commended to his people were not just to be learned patterns of behaviour, but rather an outpouring of thankfulness from the heart. David prayed, **'Keep this desire in the hearts of your people for ever, and keep their hearts loyal to you'**

(29:18). For Solomon in particular David prayed, '**Give my son Solomon the wholehearted devotion to keep your commands, requirements and decrees and to do everything to build the palatial structure for which I have provided**' (29:19).

The Chronicler took every opportunity to highlight the importance of wholeheartedness in whatever God's people do for him. If all that David has just acknowledged is true (that all that we possess comes from God) then the only appropriate response is 'wholehearted devotion'. It is from a heart at peace with God and completely devoted to him that true generosity flows. This is what the people acknowledged when they '**bowed low ... before the Lord**' (29:20).

Our gratitude to God ought to be deepened still further when we consider that God has given us 'his indescribable gift' in the person of his Son, the Lord Jesus Christ (2 Cor. 9:15). Significantly, in that same chapter Paul had much to say about giving to the Lord's work; we ought 'to give, not reluctantly or under compulsion, for God loves a cheerful giver', for material generosity is one aspect of 'the obedience that accompanies your confession of the gospel of Christ' (2 Cor. 9:7,13).

David's prayers were answered (29:21-30)

David's example, instruction and prayers were greatly used by God to mould the spiritual life of Israel. In verses 21-30 we consider the fruit of these blessed influences, for the people responded with gladness to David's pleas and acknowledged the Lord as their God.

Firstly, we read of *the sacrifices and offerings* they made before the Lord that day and note that they were made with '**great joy**' (29:21-22). The more wholehearted the commitment of God's people, the greater will be their capacity to enjoy his presence.

Secondly, we read that *Solomon was acknowledged* **'as king a second time'** while David was still alive (29:22-25). This common practice in biblical times has already been referred to and was a means of assuring a smooth succession for the chosen candidate for the throne. The first time Solomon had been acknowledged by the people as David's heir is mentioned in 23:1. In spite of the palace coup to place David's son Adonijah on the throne in the place of Solomon (described in 1 Kings 1) the affections of the people were with Solomon and he ruled with all the loyalty that David had enjoyed. If anything, Solomon enjoyed even more loyalty than David because **'The Lord highly exalted Solomon in the sight of all Israel and bestowed on him royal splendour such as no king over Israel ever had before'** (29:25).

Thirdly, the Chronicler attempts to summarize *the life of David* and describe how he was remembered after he died (29:26-30). These verses read like an obituary and show how David's memory was guarded and respected.

These three blessings were God's answers to David's prayers. In each case God used David as an instrument to bring about the answer to his own prayers. It is never sufficient to pray for a thing unless we are also willing for God to use us to pursue that end. For example, it is vain to pray for the conversion of a friend if we are not willing to speak to that person about the claims of Christ.

David had prayed for a willing people (29:17), and his generous example (29:2-5) inspired the willing spirit described in verses 21-22. David had prayed for a son to continue his work and bring it to completion (29:19; 17:23-27) and his faithfulness as a father helped to ensure that such a son was found in Solomon. Apart from his faithfulness in praying for

Solomon, David charged Zadok the priest to be Solomon's guide (29:22). David had also prayed that future generations would walk in the ways of the Lord after his death (29:18) and his reputation continued to be an inspiration for many.

One of the blessings of a godly life is that it will be remembered joyfully as a blessing to others. 'The memory of the righteous will be a blessing, but the name of the wicked will rot' (Prov. 10:7). The world can get its priorities badly out of focus, honouring scoundrels and forgetting saints. It does not honour the meek or faithful, but God does, and we need to learn to look at the world around us from God's perspective. How often have God's people despaired when they see evil men gain the upper hand! (Ps. 12:1; 73:3). The psalmist was able to find relief from his discouragement by considering the 'final destiny' of the wicked and that of the just (Ps. 73:17,27,28).

We must learn to look at people with a spiritual perspective (2 Cor. 5:16) and this means taking note of what is godly in a believer's life, learning from it and returning thanks to God for it. The book of Proverbs says of the godly woman that 'Her children will arise and call her blessed' (Prov. 31:28). Even after she has died and passed from this earth her children will carry her influence far and wide so that many who had never met her will be influenced by her and their lives will sweetened by hers.

The same is true of King David. Many generations have passed since he walked on the earth, but we are still remembering his life. God caused the events of his life to be recorded in the Scriptures so that we might learn about him — his troubles, his struggles, his prayers and his victories. The Chronicler mentions three contemporary records of David's life (29:29), and we may presume that he drew on them in writing his own history. Nathan and Gad were prophets of the Lord although their writings did not form part of the canon of Scripture.

Samuel was one of the greatest of the Old Testament prophets and his writings are better known to us, as they have been preserved for us in the Scriptures.

These written records are of great spiritual value to us. What Paul wrote about the Old Testament believers in general in 1 Corinthians 10:11 is especially true of King David: 'These things happened to them as examples and were written down as warnings for us, on whom the fulfilment of the ages has come.' His life still is able to rebuke, teach, encourage and inspire us. We are blessed by him. May God make us willing people who have been blessed and challenged by the example of one of his truly great servants.